In Love With A Monster
Life in an Abusive Relationship

In Love With A Monster

Life in an Abusive Relationship

In Love With A Monster
Life in an Abusive Relationship

In Love With A Monster

Life in an Abusive Relationship

In Love With A Monster
Life in an Abusive Relationship

In Love With A Monster
Life in an Abusive Relationship

*Trigger Warning: This book may contain triggering and/or sensitive material to some readers. Violence, sexual assault, and spousal abuse are some topics mentioned in the following chapters. If you feel triggered, please know there are resources available to help you. This book focuses on the perspective of women in abusive relationships. We understand that men are victims of domestic abuse also. In no way are we putting all the blame solely on one gender.

In Love With A Monster
Life in an Abusive Relationship

In Love With A Monster
Life in an Abusive Relationship

In Love With A Monster
Life in an Abusive Relationship

© Copyright 2022 Lena Ma

All rights reserved. No part of this publication may be reproduced, distributed, or transmitted in any form or by any means, including photocopying, recording, or other electronic or mechanical methods, without the prior written permission of the publisher, except in the case of brief quotations embodied in critical reviews and certain other non-commercial uses permitted by copyright law.

Cover Design by RJ Creatives

In Love With A Monster
Life in an Abusive Relationship

In Love With A Monster
Life in an Abusive Relationship

Table of Contents

Chapter One
Facts vs. Myths of Domestic Abuse
13

Chapter Two
What is Domestic Abuse?
18

Chapter Three
Sexual Abuse
29

Chapter Four
Psychological vs. Physical
35

Chapter Five
Male Privilege
43

Chapter Six
Empty Apologies
57

In Love With A Monster
Life in an Abusive Relationship

Chapter Seven
Are Abusers Born or Created?
64

Chapter Eight
Red Flags
71

Chapter Nine
Love Bombing & Lies
77

Chapter Ten
The Power Struggle
85

Chapter Eleven
Regret
91

Chapter Twelve
Guilt & Victim Blaming
101

Chapter Thirteen
Mental Health Issues Do Not Equal Abuse
113

Chapter Fourteen
Why Victims Stay & How They Get Trapped
120

In Love With A Monster
Life in an Abusive Relationship

Chapter Fifteen
The Barriers to Getting Free
129

Chapter Sixteen
Just Let Her Go
138

Chapter Seventeen
Stockholm or "Prisoner" Syndrome & Likelihood of Murder
153

Chapter Eighteen
When to Involve the Police
161

Chapter Nineteen
The Victim Becomes the Abuser
166

Chapter Twenty
The Deadly Nature of Continued Mental Abuse
170

Chapter Twenty-One
Desperation of the Abuser
174

Chapter Twenty-Two
Inside the Abuser's Head
183

In Love With A Monster
Life in an Abusive Relationship

Chapter Twenty-Three
Can You Love an Abuser?
189

Chapter Twenty-Four
Can He Be Forgiven?
200

Chapter Twenty-Five
Change Isn't Easy
207

Chapter Twenty-Six
The Psychological Warfare of Abuse
213

Chapter Twenty-Seven
It's Over. Now What?
222

Chapter Twenty-Eight
Premeditated Abuse: Steps Abusers Take to Hurt Others
229

Chapter Twenty-Nine
Time to Put Our Knowledge to the Test
237

Chapter One

Facts vs. Myths of Domestic Abuse

I once had a friend who would give everything she had to her husband – her heart, her time, her money, her tears, and eventually, even her life. She never saw it coming. A once fun-loving and compassionate man turned a complete 180 degrees barely two weeks after their promise under the grace of God to swear their lives to each other, to become husband and wife.

The crazy thing is, I knew her husband very well. We were best friends before their engagement and promise of holy matrimony. Sure, there were some anger issues, as there are in all living beings. But other than the occasional temper tantrum, he seemed about as normal as any other man. And she saw that. He treated my friend like a woman deserves to be treated in a relationship. He adored her every step. They were happy together, as happy as any couple could be, spending a year living as committed partners before officially tying the knot.

Judging from his exterior, nobody would have ever known that he was much more violent than anyone would have ever deemed him to be, a true monster hidden beneath a hard, shallow shell of a man. Especially not her. She loved him, so much so that she failed to see the warning signs, even though they were right in front of her face.

Each slap was followed by an excuse for his stress. Each scar was followed by an excuse of an accident. Each bruise was followed by an excuse that she deserved it. She always had a cover up for his heinous behaviors, hiding her sadness and fear behind layers of clothing and overgrown hair. As a recent graduate of an Ivy League university, she was

In Love With A Monster
Life in an Abusive Relationship

not a foolish girl. She had been careful in her relationships before, seeing signs from men who weren't right for her and quickly leaving, never turning back. But this man was different. It was as if he had cast some sort of spell over her, a spell she couldn't break out of even if her life depended on it.

As quickly as he came into her life and swept her off her feet, he grabbed her by the neck and threw her against the wall. But it was too late. She was hooked, trapped in an endless cycle of excuses and torment that she now struggled to remove herself from. A month passed. Then three months. Six months. The violence continued inside the home of Valerie Watson until the beautiful, intelligent girl I once knew met her very death at the young age of 25.

Okay, pause. Domestic abuse is a dark and disturbing topic. Not one to be taken lightly. We know that abusers are manipulators who will lie to get whatever they want. What's even more concerning is just how much their abnormal ways of thinking and acting towards women has seeped into our collective consciousness at a societal level. In this next chapter, we will see how a victim's mind gets toyed with until nothing makes sense to her anymore, or until she begins to think *she's* the crazy one! Can you separate the facts from fiction? Play along.

Myth: Domestic violence only affects women.

In Love With A Monster
Life in an Abusive Relationship

Fact: 1 in 3 women, and 1 in 4 men, are physically abused (in some way) by an intimate partner. 30% to 50% of transgender people will face domestic violence in their lifetime.

Myth: Drugs, alcohol, stress, and mental illness are the causes of domestic violence.

Fact: Although drugs, alcohol, stress, and mental illness can be factors in a life of abuse and can certainly complicate a disgusting situation, they do not lead to domestic violence.

Myth: Abusers are simply out of control and need to control their anger.

Fact: Many abusers use deliberate tactics to maintain power and control in a relationship. Sometimes, these measures can involve physical violence and aggression, but there are many other ways to overcome them.

Myth: Domestic violence is always physical abuse.

Fact: While physical abuse can be a means of maintaining power and control, it is not found in every abusive relationship, and if it does occur, it is usually not just abuse. Emotional exploitation, financial exploitation, sexual exploitation, loneliness, threats, and intimidation are all forms of domestic violence.

In Love With A Monster
Life in an Abusive Relationship

Myth: If the prey does not leave the predator, maybe their situation is not so bad, or the victim is being treated well enough.

Fact: It's hard to break a bad relationship. On average, the victim will try to leave an abusive relationship at least eight times before successfully leaving. Some tricks to make a victim stay can include: creating financial dependence, using children as a tool of oppression, and threatening violence or legal reprisals, even after the judicial system has gotten involved.

Chapter Two

What is Domestic Abuse?

When we hear the words "domestic violence," our minds tend to move toward physical abuse and, in particular, physical abuse carried out against women by the hands of men. Despite this commonly held belief, it's not always the case with violence happening inside a household. Domestic violence can occur in any form. Victims of abuse have the potential to be women, men, LGBTQ+ folks, and sadly, even children or pets. Abuse knows no age or race limits. It occurs all over the world, and no one is immune. Specifically, this book will seek to address domestic violence between men and women.

To start, we need to first talk about how domestic violence isn't limited to physical violence alone. Domestic violence is any type of abuse where the motivation of the abuser is to victimize their wife, girlfriend, companion, partner, beau, child, or relative. Ultimately, abuse is a choice. It isn't fair to claim that it is brought about by rage, mental illness, medical issues, or any other singular reason.

While these accompanying issues can certainly play a big part in learning about *why* someone might choose to abuse another human being, let us be clear: we are *not* implying causation. Having anger problems doesn't cause a person to become abusive. They consciously choose to act this way, despite their own emotions or personal demons.

Let's address another popular misconception. Presently, when the overall population imagines scenarios involving domestic abuse, they, for the most part, think about physical attacks that leave victims with noticeable wounds. This includes: cuts, bruises, broken bones, etc. At work, a colleague might notice dark purple bruising around a female coworkers' neck. Or during a family holiday dinner, maybe a worried uncle points out that his niece seems to be awfully clumsy around the house, since it seems that every time they get together, she's sporting a new cast, crutch, or arm sling.

Physical violence is often the most easily recognized by outsiders because it's just that – visible. But there are other classifications of abusive conduct beyond bodily injury. Regardless, it goes without saying that physical violence can be lethal. A victim who experiences hands-on abuse is at a higher risk of death. In fact, a UN study found that approximately 30,000 women die every year worldwide, thanks to domestic abusers. If this statistic is horrifying and leaves you feeling a ball in the pit of your stomach…good. It should.

Domestic abuse is a crime. But the drawn-out decimation of personhood that comes along with different types of abuse – like psychological – can't be ignored either.

Below, we are going to investigate the various components of abuse. The signs of domestic violence are sinister…and not always easy to see. The fact of the matter is, men have been responsible for murdering their female partners since the dawn of time. Whether we choose to acknowledge it or not, it's still happening at an alarming rate.

In Love With A Monster
Life in an Abusive Relationship

As any survivor will attest to, there are many different types of abuse. They range from mental to physical to sexual. Or a horrific combination of all three. No matter how hard a woman fights back against an abusive partner, she is already at a disadvantage because domestic abuse is rooted in male privilege (more on this later). Additional types of abuse include: disengagement, verbal, such as using coercion, threats, or blame, as well as financial abuse. But the first red flag in any abusive relationship is control.

Control is inherently involved in domestic abuse. Men who abuse others are naturally drawn to the feeling of power it gives. Men who are weak – or feel that they are perceived as weak by societal standards – gravitate toward lording power over anyone they can. This lends to a false sense of superiority and inflated importance. Never mind that only bullies prey on those less powerful than themselves.

For the abuser, it doesn't matter. We know that extremely controlling behavior is one popular path domestic abusers usually follow. Why? Well, because it's an effective way for an abuser to exert total dominance over their victim. Exercising control isn't as easy to object to as, say, a slap across the cheek. A woman who is hit by her partner might be so shocked by his actions, she immediately flees.

In Love With A Monster
Life in an Abusive Relationship

Controlling behavior, on the other hand, is frequently inconspicuous, tricky to pinpoint, and starts off slow. Over time, the obsessive controlling nature of an abuser builds up and up and up until, finally, a woman no longer recognizes just how bad the situation has become. By then, she's stuck.

Obsessive control is like a dark shadow. Always there, hovering at a woman's heels and impossible to get rid of. It might start out as something small. For example, a husband asserting that he is the one responsible for filling up the gas tank for the family vehicle. On one hand, this seems nice. How helpful! The man of the house gets the gas.

However, this oftentimes leads to more concerning control-freak habits. An abusive partner might check the mileage on the odometer after a grocery store run because they are paranoid about where their girlfriend/wife is going or who she's seeing. It could also look like limiting access to a car by hiding the keys, or withholding money to limit their access to freedom.

In one terrifying case, an abuser even went so far as to install a tracking system. A mechanic in the US posted a video during a routine check of a female client's car. When he lifted the car up to inspect the bottom, he made a gut-twisting discovery. Her ex-boyfriend had secretly placed a small tracking device by the wheel. The woman had been suspicious that she was being followed, and so this mechanic literally could have saved her life by ripping out the machine.

After this story blew up, another mechanic chimed in to say he finds similar tracking devices on women's cars "all the time." As we can see, abusers go to extreme lengths to control their victims' movements.

If you think that's scary, listen to this. Phone usage is the second most common way that abusers exert control. Yes, that's right. Even something as simple as a phone call can become deadly in a domestic abuse situation.

Abusers have been known to observe phone calls in the background or listen in on private conversations. They might demand the use of speaker phone. When their wife or partner is taking a shower, they may unlock the screen and scroll through the phone log history to read text messages. To some, this might sound like snooping. He's just a little jealous! He's just curious.

Maybe. But for a woman planning her escape and wanting to flee an abusive home, having the ability to privately communicate with social workers, shelters, and family is literally her only lifeline. Once that connection to outside help is severed, it becomes extremely dangerous to build again.

In Love With A Monster
Life in an Abusive Relationship

On the extreme end, some abusers actually regulate when a woman can make phone calls, for how long, and with whom. Not allowing a woman to own a cellphone is a perverse, but effective, way to keep her from formulating an escape plan.

In addition, abusers control the appearances of their victims. We've all been recipients of nice compliments or rude opinions. Sadly, it goes further than that. For women living with domestic abuse as a part of their daily lives, this means not being given the opportunity to decide their own fashion, style, or hairdo. Too much makeup, too little makeup...when dealing with an abuser, there's no winning.

Lastly, men who are abusive like to keep their victims on their toes. The objective? To startle. By controlling every miniscule detail of their partners' movements, but never quite pinning down their own habits with any sort of predictability, abusers make life a living hell for the women stuck with them. Which, to be perfectly honest, is their number one goal.

We can see how, in all of these examples, the abuser isolates his victim. By exerting extremely controlling behavior, an abuser forces his target to become totally reliant on him. Subjects of abuse who lose the power to make decisions about their own lives (such as simple things, like what day of the week she's allowed to go shopping or which family members she is allowed to talk to over the phone) often find that their sense of self-confidence gets warped. A victim might erroneously start to accept that, hey! Maybe my abuser is right. Maybe I really do need his permission. He's only trying to take care of me, right? Perhaps I really am unequipped to perform basic life duties without his help. Maybe my abuser really does know best.

Wrong!

In the beginning, controlling behavior may seem like love. It's not. Very soon, we see these actions take a dark turn. What once looked like adoration, suddenly transforms into possessiveness and envy. By the time a woman sees the lie for what it truly is, it's too late.

Another way that abusers press for control is through children. They might get kids to act as spies. As any woman with children knows, little eyes and ears see and hear it all. Men who abuse often get the kids to "tattle tale" on their mother by offering rewards like treats or candy or attention. In doing so, abusers hijack their innocent minds. Asking questions like, "What did mommy do today?" suddenly becomes very, very dangerous.

Next, the death of children. A horrid, despicable, wicked thing…but a truth that needs to be faced. In domestic disputes, it isn't only the woman who suffers. Every year children die at the hands of their fathers. Why? Because when the victim's parent finally decides to leave, ask for help, or call the Department of Child Safety, the abuser will react. This can take the form of threatening to harm, assault, kidnap, or even kill, the children in the marriage. Even if it doesn't go that far, abusers will still try to limit how much time the other parent can spend with her children, especially if they have separated and share custody.

As we can see, controlling behavior is insidious. It has the ability to take on many forms. Since most domestic abusers are experts in the art of manipulation, how one man decides to exert control will look vastly different from another, because research shows that manipulators know how to find a woman's weakness and use it to his advantage. Think about it. How many survivors of domestic assault have come forward and said, "If it wasn't for my children, I would have left long ago!" or "I couldn't run away. I had no money!"

The sad truth is, men who abuse can sniff out weakness like dogs on a bone. They know exactly which nerves to hit in order to keep their victims in line. For an outsider looking in, the situation might seem crazy. But for a woman who is stuck living it, the controlling behavior is justified day after day until it eventually morphs into a new – though bizarre – kind of normal.

In Love With A Monster
Life in an Abusive Relationship

Okay. So, now we have learned about control. What happens next? Does this mental manipulation carry on forever, or does it change into something worse?

The answer is…complicated.

Some women go through their whole lives like this. From the "I do's" on their wedding day to their graves, they endure this type of abuse. But for others, it gets even more horrifying. Controlling tactics soon escalate into physical violence. Physical violence manifests in different ways. For some women, it's a black eye. For others, never knowing where her next meal is coming from.

According to the AMEND Workbook for Ending Violent Behavior, physical abuse is any truly forceful conduct, the withholding of physical needs, unsafe behavior towards another person, or putting somebody else in physical danger. Not by accident! This is purposeful endangerment. It might look like: hitting, kicking, slapping, pushing, pulling, punching, beating, scratching, squeezing, hair pulling, cutting, shooting, suffocating, or attacking with a weapon of any sort. When a fight escalates beyond just verbal insults and name-calling, it's now physical abuse.

Withholding bodily needs is also a form of physical abuse. Less obvious, but equally harmful. This might look like constant interrupting of sleep patterns, not allowing rest, starvation or limiting food intake/meals, refusing access to transportation, denying cash or access to a bank account, refusing to help when a victim is debilitated or disabled, and declining to give someone access to necessities required to live a healthy life. Basically, refusing to acknowledge a woman's humanity.

That's not all. Physical abuse can also look like harming – or taking steps to harm – others. Ever seen a man kick a dog? Or backhand his son? Such actions aren't necessarily intended to hurt the child or the animal (though they for sure do!) Sometimes, abusers hurt the things a woman cares about as a way of hurting her. Harming a pet, child, personal property, or member of the woman's family is a surefire way for an abuser to get a reaction...which is exactly what he craves.

An abuser might also physically restrict his victim against her will, such as by blocking an exit or holding her down. In abuse cases, the mind becomes a prison. But quite literally, so does the home.

Chapter Three

Sexual Abuse

Sexual abuse is at the very core of so many heartbreaking domestic abuse cases. Stories abound of judicial courtrooms packed tight, only to listen to the testimony of a crying victim. Many witnesses to sexual abuse have to undergo years of therapy, just to recover from the secondhand trauma that results when you are involved in something so heinous.

In Love With A Monster
Life in an Abusive Relationship

Crimes that are sexual in nature are beyond words. And yet, we know they occur each and every day.

Sexual abuse is defined as utilizing sex in an exploitative style or forcing unwanted sexual acts on someone else. Or, to summarize, getting intimate with a partner without their outright consent. It can be as quick as being inappropriately touched on the leg during a bus ride, or as violent as rape. Consent doesn't matter. It's not even on an abuser's radar. Not remotely.

People in healthy relationships understand consent. But abusers do not. Or to be blunt, they choose to ignore boundaries. Sexual abuse might include both verbal and physical elements where consent is steamrolled. As long as the abuser gets his gratification, to him, nothing else matters.

We know abuse takes on different forms. In sexual abuse, this looks like utilizing power, compulsion, blame, and control, or not even thinking about the victim's lack of desire to engage in sexual relations. Victims might be subjected to have intercourse with others, have unwelcome sexual encounters, or be forced to take part in prostitution against their will, all because their abusers told them to. It's a highly illegal activity, but when has the law ever stopped an abuser?

In Love With A Monster
Life in an Abusive Relationship

Unfortunately, drugs and alcohol often pop up in sexual abuse cases as well. By assaulting a victim while she is inebriated, an abuser essentially takes away their victim's right to make an educated decision about sex. A woman could be asleep, drunk, sedated, or impaired. Conversely, she might simply be too young or too old to make a safe choice. Remember, legally, anyone deemed a "child" due to their age cannot give consent in the US! The same goes for anybody with a mental state that stops them from being able to safely act based on information and facts.

Similarly, an abuser might reach for a victim in a nonconsensual way. This includes touch, like undesirable penetration (oral, rectal, or vaginal) or unasked-for skin-to-skin contact (stroking, kissing, licking, sucking, the utilization of objects/toys, etc.) on any part of the victim's body.

Equally disgusting, but no less detrimental, is sexual comments directed at an uninterested party. Ever been laughed at? Or been the butt of a joke? Doesn't feel very good, huh? So, why then, do abusers think it's in any way acceptable to ridicule another's body? Because it suits their twisted needs. Chuckling at, offering hostile expressions towards, annoying, or verbally abusing a woman regarding her sexuality *is* a form of abuse.

In Love With A Monster
Life in an Abusive Relationship

We've all heard it in passing. Some gross "compliment" from a total stranger on the street that suddenly turns nasty. Catcalls from boys in passing cars. Pestering for phone numbers at the bus stop. Weird eye contact in the elevator. Sexual innuendos such as these are commonplace in the outside world, so it only makes sense that abusers will bring the same energy into their relationships at home.

Once an abuser has captured the attention of their intended victim, next, they might employ a series of tactics to reel them in closer. When alone, abusers are known to restrain a victim's contact with the outside world. They try to get women to cut off ties with family and friends. When a woman shows any interest – even if it's not romantic! – in another person, abuser's typically respond with over-the-top envy.

Jealousy raises its ugly head like a lion. Abusers roar claims of treachery or cheating. Totally unfounded! But it doesn't matter. In their minds, the poor behavior is justified because, for a millisecond, they are no longer the center of attention and in control of their victim's actions. Research has also shown that an overwhelming number of abusers can be classified as narcissists. Not terribly surprising, is it?

Imagine an abuser is angry. He believes his partner is not giving him the attention he deserves. What to do? Having illicit relationships is one answer. Try to follow along. Okay, so, in the abuser's mind, a woman has been unfaithful. In this scenario, pretend she hasn't been. She's innocent. But our abuser believes she's seeing another man. In a warped sense of reality, the abuser flies into a jealous fit. In response, they, themselves, then engage in cheating and/or affairs. This is done as a way to punish or insult their victim (who, all the while, was innocent). The result? Chaos and manipulation of facts. Which we know, an abuser thrives in.

That's one extreme. Another way they use control as an instrument, is to deny sex. Withholding affection or physical touch is damaging to our mental health. Studies carried out on primates, like gorillas and chimpanzees, in research labs tell us that social isolation leads to increased stress levels and poorer health outcomes. In short, we need to be touched! Depriving human beings of physical affection is a form of neglect. Abusers know this. Therefore, they purposely exploit this life necessity to punish those they pretend to "love."

And it succeeds. Punishment works because it's highly effective. Even incredibly intelligent woman (like the Ivy League friend I mentioned at the beginning of this book) can be tricked into accepting domestic violence. Confident, beautiful, smart people get caught in the spider's web of lies and deceit. They get worn down slowly, methodically over time, until the punishment is so absurd, so irrational, that they have lost the ability to see their abuser for who he really is – a psychopath.

In summary, sexual abuse can take many forms. It's imperative we learn how to differentiate each type in order to see the patterns as they form. If we don't, and we choose to remain blind to the realities of sexual abuse, then why would it ever stop?

Chapter Four

Psychological vs. Physical

When a baby girl is born and wrapped up in a pink blanket for the first time, no parent imagines that she will one day become the victim of abuse. When a father gives away his daughter at her wedding, he never thinks her new husband is a demon in disguise. We all want to believe that domestic abuse is something faraway. Some awful thing that only happens in bad places and to women who "deserve it." The scary reality is, domestic abuse is going on right under our noses and in our own backyards.

A book was published in 1993 that details just how bad the situation has gotten. According to the "AMEND Workbook for Ending Violent Behavior," written chiefly by Michael Lindsey, psychological mistreatment is any behavior that abuses another person's weaknesses or character. Things like persistent debasement, terrorizing, control, indoctrination, etc.

In other words, being a jerk.

Abusers who prefer psychological abuse over physical abuse are a different breed of evil altogether. They might openly insult their victim. Or try to humiliate their partner in public. We've all seen the ways a man reprimands his wife at the mall or in a restaurant over some silly thing he perceived as a mistake.

Horrified onlookers watch and wait to see...is he going to hit her? Do the police need to be called? Should a bystander intervene? In the case of psychological abuse, most oftentimes, the answer to all three of these questions is no. Hence, why psychological abuse is so deadly. It slips past us like a ghost. It is intangible. We can only hear it, but there's no blood. No broken bones. Abusers are able to completely disregard the thoughts and emotions of their victims, all the while, staying invisible to the consequences of their actions.

In more detail, psychological abuse might look like an abuser undermining or attacking (either straightforwardly or in a roundabout way) with the goal of causing mischief or misfortune. For example, threatening to murder their victim or themselves, thus, planting seeds of terror in the mind of the person they want to continue abusing.

Abusers might also play with their victim's thoughts by distorting reality. Lies become truths. Facts dissolve into nothingness. When we no longer know what's fact or what's fiction, disarray and uncertainty become a daily occurrence. This is why survivors of domestic abuse often claim their brain "was in a fog." It was! Abusers construct an insane version of reality that locks out any possibility for the victim to criticize their abuser or run free from them. When we are constantly in a state of fight-or-flight mode, we cannot think rationally.

Remember, abusers are sneaky. If one method of psychological abuse fails, they will try another. Keep an eye out for dismissive language. When a man ignores a woman's needs on purpose, we should take immediate notice. If we hear the words, "You are so stupid!" or "Why can't you ever do anything right?" and "You're an embarrassment!", then we know something is up. Telling a victim that she's dumb or clumsy works wonders. Since we know we live in a patriarchal society that values men over women, these calculated insults feed into an existing system designed to keep men in power.

When a woman calls a man *stupid*, it's an insult. However, when a man calls a woman dumb, it reaffirms the stereotype of females being less intelligent than males. Abusers *know* this. That's why they pick these specific insults to hurtle. To subvert women back down to a lower level. It's nasty, mean, and underhanded. And it works.

Ever been so drunk, you couldn't walk straight? What made you do it? While we've all gotten a tad too inebriated at an annual holiday party, driving a woman to consume medications or encouraging alcohol reliance as a method to cope with ongoing abuse is a new low. Nonetheless, survivors of abuse often report that their abuser participated in or actually prompted drug use. Sometimes, the abuser himself is an addict. By encouraging codependence, abusers are, once again, able to exert control.

Then, there's religion. All throughout history, men have used religion to undermine a woman's authority. Abusers who identify with a religion (whether it be Christianity, Catholicism, Islam, Hinduism, Judaism, or any of the thousands of others) will turn words into a weapon. Many abusers believe it is their right to beat women. They are also taught that women are subservient and, as such, can be treated like property. The fact that, in the year 2021, we *still* need to address this issue, proves just how disturbing the trend of domestic abuse is. A natural extension of this is, of course, victim blaming, secret keeping, and using any type of pressure or control that sabotages the victim's happiness, all in the name of the abuser keeping his deathly tight grip on control.

Isolation is a type of abuse firmly associated with controlling practices. It's one of numerous tools in an abuser's toolkit. By shielding the victim from seeing who they want to see, doing what they need to do, defining and meeting objectives, and controlling how the victim thinks, feels, and where she goes, the abuser is disengaging the victim from the social security net that could one day enable the victim to leave the toxic relationship. By keeping the victim socially separated, the abuser is keeping her from contact with the world.

It's like the old saying…we never truly know what happens behind closed doors. Abusers know this too. If the outside world can't see what's going on, then the abuser's convictions can't be shaken. The best way to keep a victim in the claws of domestic abuse is to hide her away from anyone who could call foul. Friends of a victim pose the biggest threat to an abuser.

In Love With A Monster
Life in an Abusive Relationship

Ever heard of love bombing? Isolation regularly starts as an outflow of a man's adoration for his victim. He will start off with proclamations like, "In the event that you truly love me, you would want to invest energy and time with me, not your family" and "If you really loved me, you wouldn't feel the need to spend so much time with your girlfriends!" As it advances, the confinement gets worse and worse, restricting or barring the victim's contact with anybody except the abuser. In the long run, the victim is disregarded completely. Without outside help, they become locked in and unable to break the chains of oppression.

Unfortunately, a few victims purposely disconnect themselves from existing support systems because they are embarrassed. We don't want people to see us at our weakest. We want to project pose and strength. How traumatizing it is to admit that a once confident woman somehow got so ensnared in an abuser's trap! Rather than admitting how badly we are hurting, how painful our wounds, we hide them. The feeling of disgrace is real. Emotional support networks can't see what's going on, and so, the abuser's actions continue on in broad daylight.

Self-detachment may, likewise, create anything from dread to open embarrassment. Fear that family will find out and any shame that might follow. As much as we hope everyone has our best interest at heart, that's simply not always the case. Victim blaming is more common than you'd think. Rather than admitting to a serious misjudgment of character, some women conceal it.

Alternatively, victim's might be worried about protecting their abuser. Seems crazy, no? But it's true. For a horde of different reasons, victims of domestic abuse don't always call the police at the first signs of violence. Sometimes, women try to paint a perfect picture of their relationship. We see this happen all the time on social media, especially on Facebook. Photos show a cheery couple in love, kissing on the beach. It can be terrifying and embarrassing to publicly admit to hundreds of followers that you were wrong about the person you thought you loved. Sometimes, it's easier to hide the truth. Keep up the fantasy, as dangerous as it may be.

What about verbal abuse? You know the classic schoolyard phrase…Stick and stones may break my bones, but words can never hurt me! Sadly, another lie.

Verbal abuse can be just as damaging as physical abuse, especially if it goes on for years and years. The stats on how many women commit suicide to escape abuse are shocking. Abusers will twist the words of their victims, causing them to question and doubt everything. Coercion, threats, blame, constant criticism over every little thing, humiliation...all drive some women to the edge.

It's a slow process, one that develops over time. What might start off as a joke, transforms into cruelty. Abusers take steps to damage a woman's self-worth by choosing specifically damning words. Common choices for ridicule include: "revolting," "bitch," "prostitute," "whore," "lazy," "bad mother," "inept," "ugly," "useless," and so on. None of these things are true, of course. A woman could be an excellent mother! One who dotes upon her children. But when an abuser wants to beat her down psychologically, he will pick the sensitive spots to "hit."

What if a victim attempts to stand up for herself? Well, then. This presents an ideal opportunity for the abuser to rage and exert ultimate dominance. It could look like shouting, rampaging around the kitchen, throwing dishes, ushering threats, or simply shutting down and refusing to talk. When an abuser knows they can't win an argument, usually, they just go AWOL. Refusal to listen to their partner's concerns is the ultimate punishment. Outsiders see it for what it is. Gaslighting. But for a victim kept in a daze of fear and confusion, verbal abuse sometimes feels like the truth.

Chapter Five

Male Privilege

How do abusers manage to accomplish so much destruction? Why don't they ever stop? Simple. The world we live in is built upon male privilege.

As long as we, as a culture, hang on to outdated male stereotypes, certain men will keep on being abusive. Don't forget! Men benefit from the current cultural system in place. Even if the man in your life has never lifted a finger against a woman, he still inherently benefits from the privilege of being assigned the gender of a male at birth. His experience in the world will automatically be vastly different than that of a woman. This is known as "male privilege." And it's not just an academic concept talked about in university lecture halls. Male privilege is a real phenomenon.

One that has deadly consequences.

Barbara Hart's "Safety for Women: Monitoring Batterers' Program" discusses this. All men profit from the violence perpetuated by abusers. Some people might not think so at first, but let us explain. When a man is violent towards a woman, it becomes the woman's responsibility to defend herself. As a culture, we shift the blame too often from where it should be (squarely on the shoulders of the abuser) and, instead, engage in a weird game of victim blaming.

We ask ourselves questions like, "Why did she put up with it for so long?" and justify the sexual assaults by saying, "Well, but how short of a dress was she wearing when she was attacked/raped? Was she drunk?" Automatically, we focus on the woman as if she is the problem. And all men benefit from this. The guy in your life might not hit you, but he, nevertheless, benefits from living in a society where men's actions are valued more than women's *reactions* to abuse.

As women, we are trained from girlhood to know that our words hold less value than those of men. So, really, is it any wonder that so many women are domestically abused each and every year? There is not a single woman who has not dreaded it, confining her exercises and her opportunities to dodge it. Women must be consistently vigilant for fear of becoming the next target. Until we rid the world of sexism, stop turning a blind eye to society's acceptance of domestic violence, and address toxic male stereotypes, male violence against women will not end.

At its core, domestic violence is about force and control. A women's activist investigation of domestic assault survivors rejects speculations that women are responsible for causing their own abuse. We've heard it all before. The endless excuses. The void justifications.

Do any of the following victim-blaming tactics ring a bell?

A man is asked why he pushed his girlfriend down a flight of stairs. In response, he says, "She stressed me out! She called me a *loser*, and I got so mad that I lost control and shoved her." In the abuser's mind, this is a valid excuse for his violence. Notice, there's no apology (there rarely is). Other excuses men use to justify their violent behaviors include: saying the woman caused monetary hardship, is too independent, too willful, doesn't listen, has a poor relationship with God, or she came from a "broken family" and doesn't know anything else except abuse. Perversely, the victim gets blamed for her own abuse. All the while, the abuser never truly admits having been the cause of any of it.

Unless he actually kills his partner, this type of abuser will carry on and on and on until, one day, the woman is either able to escape or is dead.

As any women's shelter counselor will tell you, this twisting of reality is common in the world of abusers. While these issues may be cited by abusers as reasons for their actions, we know that even if these components were erased, it would not be enough to end all men's violence against women, because they are not the root causes.

Abusers carry on viciously controlling their partner's behavior, keeping control over their partners and getting their own needs and wants met rapidly and totally. There are numerous reasons why a man might justify his actions to meet his own selfish needs. An abuser may decide to be vicious in light of the fact that he thinks that it's amusing. Some people think it's funny to scare others. In addition, a man might threaten his partner on the grounds of relationship stress or because of a disagreement in the marriage over money, children, the household, etc. Whatever suits his fancy in the moment.

Violence is a scholarly conduct, and abusers decide to utilize it. Remember, nobody forces a man to be violent. It is a conscious decision each and every single time. It's a choice. The victim isn't a part of the greater issue at hand. A victim of domestic abuse might acknowledge that they played a part in causing the abuser to "lose his temper," however, in all actuality, the abuser alone is responsible for his conduct.

As time goes on, it gets harder and harder to stay alive. Walking through life as a woman isn't for the faint of heart. We face the threats of abuse, assault, rape, and murder 365 days a year. The previous chapter looked at why a man might abuse his partner. This next part investigates five real social conditions that also contribute to men abusing women.

Right off the bat, we need to call out the commodification of women. The belief that a woman only exists as a body for the fulfillment of a man's sexual and physical needs isn't just uncivilized – it's dangerous. Historically, it wasn't that long ago that women were considered property. They had about the same rights as a donkey or a cow (and in many parts of the world, young girls are still bought and sold as commodities). Bride trafficking is a multimillion-dollar business. In some countries, children as young as ten are married to men three or four times their age. So, clearly, the days of treating women as bodies first and people second are not over. Is it any wonder then, that this social condition leads to the abuse of women by the hands of men?

We already talked about male privilege, but it's worth mentioning again, if only for the sake of building this argument. When males are given positions of authority, society expects the control, pressure, and rebuffing of female autonomy. Men who support women are often seen as breaking ranks with their fellow men. This is the evil face of male privilege. Men will not disrupt the status quo, lest it risks their own privilege.

The belief that physical power is worthy of admiration and signals success contributes to this. Men are naturally bigger, stronger, and taller compared to women. To be different, is to be wrong. So, while male privilege hurts women; we must also recognize that it hurts non-conforming men too.

In a way, this all has a lot to do with cultural stigma. Cultural stigmas that do nothing to dissuade a man's predominance for his controlling and assaultive behavior. By neglecting to step in and forcefully say, "this is wrong" when they see abuse happening, some people of specific cultural upbringings essentially put a stamp of approval on the violence occurring in their own communities.

And it is possible to say, "Enough!" Actor Ian Somerhalder is well-known for his anti-violence charity work. He says, "It's so easy to forget the many women who live their lives in fear because of domestic violence. Men have an important role to play in sending out the message that real men do not hurt or abuse their partners."

Finally, financial abuse. This is the last social condition that contributes to men abusing women. Financial abuse is an approach to monitoring the victim through the control of monetary assets. This usually means controlling the family salary, not permitting the victim access to cash, or restricting access to family reserves. This might also include: keeping concealed records, secret bank accounts, not telling a partner about investment gains and losses, not letting a victim have any say in how money is spent, allotting a weekly/monthly spending "allowance" for basic life necessities like food or feminine hygiene products, forcing a working victim to hand over their paychecks, or refusing to allow the victim to get a job so she can earn her own income.

At its absolute worst, financial abuse can also take the form of an abuser calling/annoying the victim at their place of work, showing up unexpectedly to "check on them," or refusing to give them access to transportation to get to work. As we can see, domestic abuse crawls into every crack of daily life. For a victim, there's no hiding. There's just surviving to see another day.

Now, we know how abuse manifests. But what do the numbers really say? In order to better understand the scale of people who suffer from domestic violence, we need to investigate the statistics and research. While reading the following paragraphs, please keep in mind that these numbers might seem underwhelming. That's because it takes a long time for survivors to come forward and document their experiences (it takes an average woman seven tries before she eventually leaves her abuser). Even then, it's estimated that most cases of domestic abuse actually go unreported. As high as these stats are, the sad truth is that they are probably much greater than anyone can even begin to imagine.

It's a hard pill to swallow. Some women have been suffering since an age as young as 16. And because they are so young, these individuals may be at further risk for future abuse (such as those who recently parted ways in the same relationship, the risk of being involved with another abuser, etc.).

Even more frightening? Most domestic abuse cases go unreported. In the year 2018 in New York alone, more than 250,000 calls came in at the New York

In Love With A Monster
Life in an Abusive Relationship

Police Department over domestic violence complaints. Even that number is likely a vast undercount. Fear holds many victims back from reporting their abusers, and so, experts in the field of domestic abuse estimate that as much as 50% - 80% of violence actually never gets reported. For the women who deal with violence as a normal part of their everyday lives, it's impossible to ignore. Yet, we all carry on about our business as if violence isn't a dark enemy seeping into our homes, our workplaces, and our communities. One has to wonder...how bad is it going to get before we do something?

The National Organization for Women (NOW) has been working for 30 years to end the domestic violence epidemic. This group states that domestic violence happens everywhere, even in the most unexpected places. Who would have ever guessed that it could happen in a church, a locker room, in a courtroom, or in the police force, where girls, teenagers, and women are being targeted? But the numbers don't lie. Abuse against women is out of control.

RAINN, a similar organization, guesses that one American is sexually assaulted every 73 seconds! Do the math. With a phone line operational 24/7, RAINN is the go-to sexual assault hotline for thousands of US women (and men). Many people are quick to point out that assaults aren't just limited to women, and to that point, they would be correct.

However, women make up an enormous majority. According to RAINN data, 9 out of every 10 victims of rape are women. Men make up just 10%. Similarly, 1 out of every 6 American women has been the victim of an attempted or completed rape in her lifetime. Rape is the most eye-catching headline in sexual assault cases. However, sexual harassment, incest, stalking, indecent exposure, voyeurism, cyber harassment, revenge porn, and trafficking all fall under the umbrella of sexual abuse.

So, the facts are in. Women are overwhelmingly more at risk of being abused domestically than men are. Clearly, the fear of walking alone at night isn't some irrational boogeyman fantasy. These are documented cases, each backed up by a living, breathing woman. One who now has to spend the remainder of her life wondering – why me? To the abuser, the question is, why not?

We can examine the US statistics to no end. But the nitty gritty reality is that some women are more at risk of being abused than others. A few factors we must address. First, economics. It's proven that people with a low income are more at risk for intimate partner violence. That is not to say wealthy people don't abuse/become abused too. They sure do. It's easy to draw the conclusion that people who are rich are morally superior to people who are poor, and that's why lower income earners experience higher rates of abuse…because they are more likely to be "bad people." This is categorically false! Not true. Not in the slightest.

The real fact of the matter is that being poor means a woman has less avenues available for her to escape an abusive partner. With a minimum wage job, or no money of her own, plus possible children to look after, it's nearly impossible for a survivor of domestic abuse to leave without some kind of financial help. Instead, they stay. Even when this decision puts her life at risk. Even when she knows death is a possibility. Being economically dependent on a man is a trap some people never escape. Ever.

Jen Rollins knows this better than anyone. She was married for 14 years to a man who was financially and verbally abusive. In an interview with Local Love, she shares, "He kept telling me that I couldn't leave. I had two young daughters at the time. Would I be able to stay in my house? Would I be able to make it financially? He told me that he would take the kids, and that I'd never hear from them again. He had isolated me from most of my friends and family, and he kept telling me that I was alone, and no one would help."

She's not alone. In Australia, when asked why she didn't apply to jobs and "just leave him," a survivor named Sapphire explains, "It's not like someone who'd just been abused can go out and work. Abuse fucks you up." She later admits in the Every Day article that the fear of not being able to make it on her own held her back. Survivors often feel alone. As if the struggle they are going through is somehow unique to them. Of course, it isn't. But this is one of the many damaging lies abusers will tell a woman about herself. That she is weak. Dependent. Incapable of change. The mental damage alone takes years of therapy to undo.

The problem is, we don't talk about the issue. Not until it's on the news. Only when a woman in our very own neighborhood is murdered by her partner do we wake up and spot what's really going on. Until then, she's just another statistic.

As we can see, there is a temptation to talk about domestic abuse in only numerical terms. However, it's crucial to remember that behind every percentage are real-life people. The above stats were intended to be a small taste of just how prevalent the issue is not only is the US, but all across the globe.

Aside from personal stories and statistics, medical research depicts domestic violence in a few different ways. It identifies with the exploitation of an individual with whom the abuser currently has, or has in the past, a casual, spousal, or sentimental connection. People who commit acts of domestic violence use coercive practices to force authority over another person, which could be an adult or even an adolescent. These practices, which can happen in private or in public, only once or progressively, include psychological mistreatment, physical violence, and nonconsensual sexual conduct.

Domestic violence is an extreme issue all over the world. It destroys the fundamental human rights of being a woman and often results in injury or death. While insights contrast delicately, women are victims of domestic violence in an essentially higher extent when contrasted with men. In the U.S., the Department of Justice reports that from 1994–2010, 4 out of 5 casualties were women in domestic violence.

The World Health Organization (WHO) states that 38% of all women killed will have been murdered by their life partner, but the watchdog admits to the fact that this is likely an underestimation. It further reports that 42% of women who had been explicitly or truly mishandled by their partners were physically harmed in detrimental ways. Numerous individuals see domestic violence as only a piece of certain ethnic or racial networks, or as limited to specific classes, inside their social orders. We like to believe that abuse doesn't happen elsewhere. In other countries. To other people who don't look or sound like "us." This simply isn't true. Domestic abuse happens everywhere. There is no land border, culture, race, or other defining description where domestic abuse isn't an issue worthy of our attention.

To back up this claim, let's review another study. In interviews that The Advocates for Human Rights led all through the CEE/FSU locale, for instance, individuals regularly examined domestic violence as far as the race, ethnicity, class, training level, or age of the abuser or victim.

It concluded that domestic violence happens in all social, financial, and cultural settings.

Chapter Six

Empty Apologies

People make up all kinds of excuses to justify their abusive behavior. To normal ears, the words ring empty. A woman who hasn't been abused listens and shakes her head in confusion. How could anyone fall for these tricks? It's so obvious he's lying. But to a victim caught up in a whirlwind of abuse (which may have been going on for years, or even decades), the excuses sound like facts.

For example, some men apologize. By profusely saying, "I'm sorry," followed by a promise of, "I won't ever do that again...," abusers hope to trick their victims into forgiving the abuse. But like the age-old phrase goes, actions speak louder than words. No matter how genuine the apology may seem, sooner or later, the words fade to dust, and the abuse raises its ugly head again. It can be challenging to see the truth, especially when love is involved. On the off-chance that you have known somebody who is abusive to their partner, you've most likely also heard the pitiful line, "I'm heartbroken." Make no mistake – this isn't an expression of remorse. Rather, it's, yet again, an attempt to legitimize the unfortunate activities that might have included physical, mental, emotional, or sexual abuse.

So, why do we acknowledge an abusive partner's expressions of remorse again and again and again? What could a victim possibly have to gain from endlessly forgiving? Well, sometimes, the defenses sound rational. Especially if the victim is searching for something – anything – to explain how the person she loves could ever act so horribly towards her. The human brain looks for patterns. It's the way our species is programmed. When things don't make sense, our brains try to find a solution, a reason why, a logical explanation. Abuse is entirely unreasonable, and yet, because the victim's relationship with her abuser is usually a long and complex one, she will try to rationalize it in any way she can. Suddenly, his lies seem okay! He promised it will never happen again. He said he was sorry, so, he must be. Right?

Wrong. Abusive partners are gifted at compulsion and control. Statements of regret can, in and of themselves, be a type of control; they make a woman fall for the trick of believing an abusive partner accepts that what he did was genuinely off-base. Think of it as a disturbing exercise in mental gymnastics. Here's what happens. First, a partner does something wrong, like hurl a glass dish at his wife's head...As she runs upstairs to the bedroom and locks the door behind her, the abuser quickly realizes that the situation is escalating. "Oh, no!" he thinks. Maybe this time, she will finally leave. What if she calls her sister for help? Or the police? The abuser begins to panic. His world is unravelling.

So, what does he do? He realizes that saying "I'm sorry" will cause him to appear contrite. Eyes filled with watery, remorseful tears, he quietly knocks on the door and laments about his grievous actions, all the while, secretly knowing that, as long as he can secure forgiveness from his victim, she will confide in him once more, and thus, allow him to keep carrying on with the abuse. It's a trick as old as time. And it never ends.

That's one way to do it. But there are other underhanded ways to keep the abuse going too. Another common tactic is based on the notion of a psychological term called "projection." Instead of confronting himself as the main problem, an abuser will turn the tables. For instance, a partner would come up with reasons to cause you to feel like what's going on is *your* issue, not theirs. It's classic blame-shifting.

For example, imagine an abusive man punches a hole in the wall. In response, a female victim might find it reasonable to yell back in fear and anger, and end up calling her abuser "crazy." Suddenly, the damaged drywall is no longer the main issue. Enraged at being called a name and talked back to, the abuser now swaps the abuse around to make his actions less important, and the woman's *reactions* the real problem. "It's not me," he argues. "It's you." That's the lie he desperately wants her to believe. Obviously, we know that being abusive is a decision. There is no justifiable reason for abusing anyone. Period. But this projection tactic is an abuser's way of asserting his self-given godlike authority. A woman might argue that she isn't in the wrong, and in fact, the man is the guilty party. But it falls on deaf ears.

However, criticism and sensible questioning don't stop most abusers. They will say anything to sustain their abusive behaviors. Ever heard of this one?

In Love With A Monster
Life in an Abusive Relationship

"Don't blame me! It's not my fault. I was drunk. I was using drugs. It wasn't the real me." Both on television shows and in legal courtrooms, criminals love to blame booze or narcotics for their poor actions. But utilizing medication or liquor isn't an excuse for being abusive. There are plenty of individuals who drink but don't beat up their wives. Ask yourself: how should a boyfriend/husband act when he's drunk around his friends? How does he behave? And, finally, how does he treat a woman when he's sober? If there is a noticeable difference between how a drunk man relates to men vs. women, this isn't an addiction issue anymore...it's a misogynistic and abusive one.

Any addictions' counselor knows that connection doesn't suggest causation. Just because two things happen together (such as drinking and violence), doesn't mean that one causes the other. To blame alcohol or drugs for abuse is like blaming a gun for murder. At the end of the day, somebody made the conscious decision to pull that trigger.

In addition, an abuser might try to say one of the following. He could shout, "I only behave this way because I care about you!" But acting extremely jealously, controlling, possessively, or violently is not an acceptable way to show someone that you care about them. These behaviors do not have any place in a healthy relationship. Likewise, an abuser might claim, "Well, you made me mad/provoked me, and I had no other choice. I can't control it." That's a lie. Stress and anger may coincide with abusive behavior, but they don't cause it, the same as we learned about the effects of drinking or taking drugs. Actions – good or bad – are always a choice.

Think about it...how does a man react when he's mad at other people? Is he going to fly off the handle at his teacher? What about his boss? Chances are low. Why? The answer is easy. An abuser knows that in these situations, they cannot get away with that kind of deplorable behavior without invoking some serious consequences in return. So, they save it for somebody less powerful who will accept their nonsense – like a girlfriend or wife.

"But...but...I have a mental illness or personality disorder!" an abuser cries. "I'm bipolar. I have PTSD." Does this excuse it? Well, not quite. Research illustrates that lots of people who have mental health issues do not behave abusively towards their partners. If an abusive partner is legitimately dealing with a mental illness or disorder, a woman needs to ask herself: are these issues affecting any part of the abuser's life, other than his relationship with me? Are they acting abusively towards people outside the relationship? If not, mental health problems alone simply cannot be used as an excuse to condone violence.

In Love With A Monster
Life in an Abusive Relationship

The last line an abuser may try to use to pull the wool over a victim's eyes is childhood trauma. A man might try to excuse his actions by saying, "I grew up in a violent home where I experienced or witnessed abuse." Maybe his dad hit his mom. Or there was a cruel grandparent. Regardless, many people have grown up in violent homes, but they choose not to abuse their partners. Actually, the opposite is true! Lots of people who have experience in abusive upbringings even go so far as to use their past as a motivation to be a healthy partner because they know how terrifying it is to be trapped in a toxic environment. Therefore, we see that, no matter what kind of trauma someone has endured in their life, abuse is never okay. It's always, always a choice.

People often have difficulty understanding the motives of those involved in abuse. Why people abuse others is a common question. And as an extension, why do people who are being abused choose to put up with it? None of these questions have easy answers. Even with the hardest effort to educate themselves, many people are never able to understand these seemingly irrational choices. It is important to live and experience the situation of abuse before internal logic begins to make any sense. However, we can do our best to understand, if only for the sake of thousands of victims who have lost their lives as a result of domestic abuse.

Chapter Seven

Are Abusers Born or Created?

The first question, "Why do people abuse others?" There is more than one answer. Some abusers have learned to abuse from their parents. Their early history includes self-abuse and/or seeing others abuse (for example, one parent abusing another or their sibling). As a result, the normal state of their lives is inherently abusive. Such people triggered a special relationship, the complementary role of "abuse" and "victimization." The abuser (this could be a father, grandfather, brother, or uncle) is well aware of the horrors he is causing. As an adult, a victim of childhood abusive experiences later fully understands it. But unlike being a childhood victim, adults have the brain capacity to choose or not choose abuse.

Because of their experiences as victims, some men prefer to take on the role of abuser once they grow up. When they reach adulthood, they simply turn the relationship around, and as they learn, they begin to take on the "abusive" side of the relationship as opposed to the "victim" side. By acting aggressively, they gain the first sense of overcoming their destiny and not being at the mercy of others. The fact that they hurt others in the process isn't even on their radar. It's a far-off, dim part of their awareness. Why be a sheep when you can be a wolf?

Abuse doesn't just have physical origins. It can also result in mental health problems or disorders. For example, anger management issues, intermittent explosive disorder diagnoses, or alcohol and drug anxieties can easily spin out of control during arguments. Those who abuse verbally or physically attack their partners and dependents do so not merely because of their mental health issues, but because they are abusers at heart. They're sick, mean, callous individuals.

In Love With A Monster
Life in an Abusive Relationship

And yet, other people abuse because they simply have a total lack of empathy. This could be either because of some kind of brain disorder or because they experienced abuse themselves as children. Their innate empathy never developed properly. Such abusers cannot relate to other people as individuals, nor will they choose to treat them as such.

Victims become objects. Abusers confuse human beings for inanimate things. They treat people as if they are there for their convenience and do not live an independent, important life. Abusers who treat people this way are very mentally ill and, possibly, medically ill. They may have a social (psychopathic) or addictive personality disorder and may include anger or impulsiveness control and substance abuse. Furthermore, some people may abuse for the sake of benefits, such as sexual or financial gratification, or the naivety of holding power over other people's lives. More on that later.

Think of a dictator who breaks your psyche. You can recognize that kind of person (for example, Saddam Hussein easily comes to mind). Or we can turn our attention to the media for examples. The role of Tony Soprano in HBO's television series, "The Sopranos," is a prime model of this. Just look at Tony's character. What makes it so interesting is that he is well aware of his tendency towards being a narcissistic sociopath, but he also struggles at different times with varying rates of success in the fight against it.

Childhood trauma accounts for the origin of many abusers. Almost all children experience traumatic events in one place or another. Maybe a bully at school. Or the loss of a much beloved pet dog. Although children do suffer after a traumatic event, most kids are resilient. Children can snap back into their regular routines in a relatively short amount of time, granted they have access to emotional support systems. With the right therapy, most children who experience abuse go on to live happy and healthy lives. Not to mention, some children are just less affected by traumatic situations than others. But experiencing abuse as a child and never healing, is a different story.

Adults who lived through negative childhood abusive experiences are more likely to report higher levels of mental health problems as parents, researchers have found. However, mental health and behavior factors only explain about a quarter of a child's high behavioral health risks. Exactly how a child's behavior is transferred from negative childhood experiences to parenthood, is an area deserving of further study.

We simply don't know enough yet. But really, what we do know is this. Studies have shown evidence that confirm what parents of abused children, or grownup victims of abuse, have been saying all along. Kids who get abused are at higher risk for continued abuse during the adult course of their lives. Researchers have used information from a national survey that looked at four generations of American families. These reports found that where there was abuse, there was also a later increase of neglect, family tension, behavioral issues, as well as attention deficit disorders. One quote taken from a study reads, "If we can identify children who are at high risk, we can link them to services that help reduce their risk or prevent behavioral health problems." So, supports do exist. To what degree they are accessed, however, remains a topic of debate.

With this data, researchers were then able to find strong relations between parents' distress and their children's behavioral health issues, while controlling for factors such as family poverty and education levels.

Consider the following case study.

Sophie is an 8-year-old Caucasian girl who has lived with her aunt, Helen, for the past five months. Helen is determined to take care of Sophie and is looking for custody. Sophie's attitude soon grows, and Helen is finding it more difficult to take care of her and seeks support. Sophie constantly asks Helen if she will live with her forever. Sophie has moved around with many different relatives and family friends since she was removed from her birth parents at the age of 2. She went back when she was 3, and she recently was removed again a year ago. In her early years, she was exposed to a unique and violent environment. Her mother was in a transition home when she was born and soon disappeared as her parents were re-arrested for some time after her father had warrants for his arrest. Sophie hasn't seen her father at all for the past year. In the care of her mother, she moved around a lot, and her mother had many different men entering and leaving the household.

What does this tell us about children who grow up in abusive environments?

Well, we know that children with PTSD may experience recurrent trauma to their brains. They can either avoid anything that reminds them of the trauma, or they can re-experience the trauma. Sometimes, children think they have lost warning signs that predict traumatic events. To avoid future trauma, they are constantly on the lookout for signals that something bad is about to happen again. As a result, children who live in violent homes often display anxiety. They might chew their nails. Or pace endlessly. Furthermore, children with PTSD may also have problems with anger or aggression. It's not uncommon for an abused child to hit/pick on fellow peers at schools as a means of coping with their feelings.

In a similar vein, some kids develop self-destructive behavior mechanisms, such as cutting, hair pulling, or scratching. Feeling isolated and alone, children grow depressed. They might find it increasingly difficult to form healthy relationships with friends or teachers and have trouble trusting others. Since verbal abuse almost always accompanies physical abuse, low self-esteem can also be an issue. For a child growing up in an abusive environment, confidence plummets. Is it any wonder? Most adults need external support and help to grow beyond their abusive partners. Imagine being a child locked into such a horrible situation. As much as women are victims, we cannot forget the millions of children worldwide who are also silently crying out for help.

Chapter Eight

Red Flags

Abusers are evildoers, not dumb. They are aware of what they are doing and follow the same blueprint in their quest to exert dominance over others. Their violence is planned and premeditated. As such, it's easy to see that abusers (as a group) have a tendency to share certain characteristics. To an innocent observer, these characteristics might seem oversimplified. However, victims of abuse, and those who have grown up in abusive households, know just how dangerous a combination of these characteristics can be.

One such trait is criticism. An abuser always notices your little doings here and there. He will criticize a woman on these little things. And really, it could be anything! The songs you like. The way you organize a cupboard. How you do your hair. It's absurd. The issue that the abuser is bringing to light isn't the point. No. Their goal is to cause friction in the relationship.

Similarly, an abuser is often very sensitive about monitoring movements. Abusers have a tendency to complain that a woman is not faithful. Claims of cheating are widespread (even without any concrete evidence). For example, an abuser may stop his victim from meeting her friends or going to school with classmates. As mentioned previously, many domestic abusers also share the characteristic of being drug/alcohol addicted. Alcohol makes the abuser more sensitive, to the point where he may become livid over nothing.

Abusers also hold money in their hands and control all the money their dependents spend. Abusers humiliate victims in front of others. The abuser takes hold of private property – like cellphones – and all the things that a woman he is violent towards cares

In Love With A Monster
Life in an Abusive Relationship

about. Often, abusers threaten that they will hurt, or even kill, victims or children or pets. Lastly, abusers use weapons against the victims. Horrifically, many domestic abusers are similar in that, as their violence escalates, they frequently go from physical attacks such as hitting, to committing sexual assaults against their victims. There are many warning signs of possible violence.

Red flags are everywhere. And yet, the signs that domestic abuse will soon occur often go willfully unnoticed. As a society, we bury the truth. Don't air dirty laundry. It's a private family matter. The neighbor's screams are none of our business. These are the lies we tell ourselves in order to avoid the terrifying reality of just how bad domestic abuse has gotten. For some unfathomable reason, there seems to be a certain naivety surrounding the prevalence of abusers.

"How could someone be so cruel?" we wonder. Surely, the stats about sky-high cases of boyfriends and husbands slaying their girlfriends or wives are exaggerated. Alas, no. While murder is on the extreme end of abuse, the road is dotted with red flags. For example, a man punching his fist through a wall. This isn't anger. This is a warning sign that this individual is capable of brutal physical violence. The destruction of items or objects proves that an abuser cannot control his emotions or places zero value in preserving a sense of peace within the home.

In Love With A Monster
Life in an Abusive Relationship

Victims of abuse often report that their abuser broke tables, chairs, electronics, or slammed doors so hard they banged off the hinges. When an abuser starts hitting or throwing things, it's a sign that the potential for physical assault is escalating. Today, it was a hole in the drywall. Tomorrow, it might be a black eye.

Likewise, we can look an abuser in the face and see the red flags. When an argument goes from raised voices to out-of-control shouting and screaming, it's another warning signal of possible domestic violence. Common sense tells a woman to always be aware of her safety needs in all interactions involving an abuser. Survivors talk about how they were told to not meet privately with an abuser, and if she must do so, make sure someone is available nearby if she needs to call for help. But as well-intentioned as all this advice is, for a woman who is trapped in a current domestic violence lifestyle, hindsight is 20/20. Warning signs are like traffic lights. Yes, they're there to help keep us all safe. But unless everybody driving on the road pays attention, what good are they? For the abuser, a red stoplight means zip. He'll continue hitting, punching, screaming, provoking…until one day, there's nothing left to attack.

Domestic abusers like to use physical force during arguments. Why? Because men are bigger and stronger than women (generally speaking). Often, men will use verbal threats too as a means to terrorize their victim into inertia. This may come across as phrases like, "Shut up, or else I will slap you across the face!" and "Say anything to the police, and I'll kill you" or "If you attempt to run away, I will track you down and break your neck." Like a big bad wolf, abusers try to become menacing. But once the heat of the moment cools off, suddenly, a shift occurs. Remember, abusers are clever! They will do and say anything to manipulate a situation to suit their false narrative. For instance, in many parts of the world, abusers use gender stereotypes to justify their actions.

Abusers will try to be forgiving for this atrocious behavior by saying that they were raised to hold strict stereotypes about the roles of men and women. The abuser may see women as inferior to men, stupid and incapable of being fulfilled without male companionship. Others are very controlling because they believe that their victims are lesser than them, and as such, cannot make smart choices for themselves or the family. This belief system can be so toxic, it escalates to a point where victims are not allowed to make any personal decisions.

Check out this example. John has a problem with his anger. All his life, he has become angry and abusive very fast. His father acted this way towards his mother, often belittling her aspirations and acting both verbally and physically abusive in the household. Nobody ever spoke up, and so, it was treated as acceptable in their tightknit community. As a result, John learns to follow in his father's footsteps once he becomes an adult. When his own wife goes to the market one day and returns home late, John grows enraged with his wife and argues with her. Then, when he feels his wife is not taking his worries seriously, he threatens to slap her across the cheek and further threatens her with physical abuse as punishment for what he perceives as a slight against his manhood. And when he senses his threats are not working, and his wife is acting outside of his gender norms belief system? The violence intensifies.

Chapter Nine

Love Bombing & Lies

Ah, falling in love. What a wonderful feeling. For many, the process of seeking a life partner is full of ups and downs, magical moments, and the occasional heartbreak. Getting involved in a relationship can be quick. Sometimes, two people just "click." They hit it off right away and start dating. There's nothing inherently wrong with this!

In Love With A Monster
Life in an Abusive Relationship

But sadly, lots of women rush into relationships before really doing their homework about who exactly it is they are interested in. This isn't necessarily their fault – as we know, abusers are masters at putting on a mask and deceiving their prey. Nonetheless, it's a fact that both men and women oftentimes enter new relationships having unrealistic (and sometimes idealistic) expectations.

Vulnerable women tend to have experienced some form of abuse before, whether from a parent, sibling, or partner. Their history of being in abusive situations romantically often stems from knowing their partner for less than six months before becoming engaged or living together for the first time. Imagine it. You've just been introduced to the man of your dreams. He's handsome, kindhearted, gets on well with your family members, and seems to be totally head-over-heels in love with you! Together, you begin talking about the future. Heck, you might even start shopping for wedding rings. Everything is bliss. Until one fateful day, he says/does something out of the ordinary that causes you to pause for a second.

What do we mean by this? Well, it could be any sort of thing. For example, a would-be abuser may make an off-hand comment and say something like, "If you love me, I need all of you. I want all your care and attention, so stop spending so much time doing x, y, and z." On the surface, this might look normal.

In Love With A Monster
Life in an Abusive Relationship

But then other weird behaviors start to accompany the comments. So-called "playful" force may be used during sex, and/or sexual fantasies may be practiced in which the victim feels helpless. This is more than kinky whims we're talking about here! Victims of newly-formed domestic abuse relationships report feeling afraid in the bedroom, being forced to do sexual favors against their will or that they are extremely uncomfortable with. Abusers can use sex as a means to legitimately endanger their victim's health, all the while, pretending it's his way of showing "love."

In regards to "pillow talk," they might say things that are deliberately cruel and painful about a victim's appearance so that her feelings are undermined and humiliated. Claiming his needs are not being met sexually, or that his wife/girlfriend doesn't satisfy him anymore, is one way abusers use sex to gain dominance. Make no mistake! Just like with all aspects of an abuser's profile, reason and logic are absent. Men who abuse are temperamental and unpredictable. Explosive mood swings are common. Rational, commonsense thinking does not exist, and so long as the ends justify the means (in the abuser's mind), physical, verbal, and sexual assaults are perfectly fine. Even when she says no. Even when she cries and begs for him to stop. To the abuser, it's all meaningless.

In Love With A Monster
Life in an Abusive Relationship

A pattern is forming. Yet again, we see sex being used as a controlling tactic. When verbal abuse is no longer getting the results an abuser wants, or when a victim stops taking the threat of violence seriously, we see the abuser flip a mental switch. Give the example below a read.

Miss "A" is 28 years old and has been married for just one year. She and her husband had a loving marriage, despite each respective family's opposition. Therefore, Miss "A" was not accepted by her in-laws and extended family members, but the couple was still allowed to live with the groom's family. Miss "A" was frequently insulted and criticized by her mother-in-law who continuously grumbled about her daughter-in-law's behavior, incapability, and unworthiness to run a family unit.

One time, the mother called her son separately to talk in private. She said that his wife was not doing any household work, goes out without her permission, and uses rude language when speaking with her. As a result, when the husband returned back home, his behavior was rude and insulting to his wife. She was not allowed to visit or meet with her parents and was threatened with a divorce. When the wife spoke out about how unfair and unreasonable this was, the husband hit her.

In this case study, we can see quite clearly how the concept of "falling in love" or having what some cultures refer to as a "loving marriage" quickly descended into a domestic abuse scenario. Where were the red flags? Did Miss "A" spot them? Or were they so well-hidden and protected by the groom's family that nobody could ever have guessed just how horribly he was capable of acting?

Aggressive or abusive behavior usually begins at home. It comes from a yearning to pick up and enforce power over another who is weaker than yourself. It might start off as picking on a little sister. Or stealing money from an elderly grandmother who has lost the ability to speak with age. Abusers see a potential weakness, and bam! They seize the opportunity. Limiting or monitoring others is a form of control. Abusers will use damaging strategies to erode equity in the home and, slowly but surely, eat away at any authority their victims ever held in the relationship.

Individuals who abuse aren't always married. While we usually think of domestic abuse in the context of a nuclear family, it occurs in the dating scene too. Maybe the boyfriend truly doesn't know that how he's behaving is abusive, especially if he's young. Perhaps they think they know best. Or that, as a man, it's their right to be in control of the relationship. Perhaps, it's just how he grew up. In his mind, everything is perfectly fine. But it's not. Eventually, someone, somewhere, at some time, is going to point out that the abusive tendencies he has and the way he is acting towards women is not acceptable in mainstream society.

The real question is…what's he going to do afterwards? Will he be disgusted by his actions and vow to change? Or will he defend himself? Tragically, numerous individuals who are raised by abusive parents choose to carry on in their parents' footsteps and continue with negative and destructive behavior. We know that abuse is a decision, one that is consciously made. Anybody can have it in them to become a monster. Sex, age, race…everybody's got an inner demon. For people who choose to engage in domestic abuse, they welcome the beast.

We all want to be loved and respected. Obviously! It's the basic requirement for any healthy relationship. The rules of the game are simple. Don't say cruel things. Do not physically assault the girl you care about. The bar couldn't possibly be lower. Young people everywhere seeking sound connections buy into the idea of true love, and yet, so many of them wind up trapped in endless cycles of domestic abuse because they fail to see the red flags. In the case of our theoretical "Miss A," the signs were all there; she just couldn't see them until it was too late.

Let's have a look at the pages below to get a deeper understanding of how exactly abuse functions, once the disease has taken root in a relationship.

In Love With A Monster
Life in an Abusive Relationship

Abusers have a disorder. Where and when they first learn how to treat other human beings so poorly, no one knows. Ask a hundred people if there are any acceptable reasons to hit a woman, and you will likely get a variety of different answers. But the one thing we can all agree on is this: abusers get a kick out of seeing others in pain. They gain joy from torment, and considerably more so when they are the ones dispensing the anguish. For them, abuse is an unfortunate chore. They abuse others to increase their own perverse individual delight.

It could be that they were abused themselves, as previously explored. Some abusers act out their dysfunctional behavior on others because it was done to them. In a subconscious effort to resolve their own abuse, they do the same to another person. This type of abusive behavior is identical, meaning it matches almost exactly to their childhood experience. The other side of this equation is that they act in an opposite way of the abuse that was done to them. However, in this case, the victim is the opposite. For instance, a boy who is sexually abused by a man might grow up to sexually abuse girls as evidence that they are not homosexual.

The reverse can be true as well. Conversely, maybe they watched something. With the advances in technology come additional exposure at a young age of glorified abuse. Some movies, songs, TV shows, and video games minimize abuse by making fun of it or making it seem normal. A typical example is verbally attacking another person by name-calling or belittling them in an online chatroom. Harmless boyhood fun? Or the unfortunate beginnings of a highly abusive future?

Chapter Ten

The Power Struggle

Guess what? The bizarre truth of the matter is that abusers feel powerless. Yes, it's true! They bully and berate women under a guise, but the reality can't be hidden. More and more people are becoming aware of just how many women are murdered in cold blood each and every year by the hands of men. One thing they all have in common is that their goal is to gain control over who they conceive of as their "prey." This is because they do not feel that they have personal power, regardless of any worldly success at their job, in their home life, or with their friends and family. Abusers are weak men who all share similar characteristics. They often have the following personality profile.

To start, they are insecure. This might be about their appearance, finances, abilities, etc. They have unrealistic expectations of a relationship, thinking everything should be picture-perfect or that women need to conform to misogynist gender roles. This is usually accompanied by a deep distrust of independent women. Abusers get jealous easily. If a man sees his girlfriend or wife chatting with another male coworker, he might take this as a personal attack, even though it's a perfectly normal occurrence and in no way indicative of cheating.

Abusers love to verbally manipulate others and make them feel less than ideal. It's a way of beefing up their own authority and power. Slurs, name-calling, curses...from morning until night, an abuser will find ways to slip verbal abuse into everyday language until it begins to sound okay to a victim's ears, or worse, she starts to believe the lies. Once this is accomplished, abusers will then find ways to separate a partner from her friends and family. Any backtalk or questioning of the abuser's words is taken as a betrayal. He's hypersensitive and reacts aggressively when his words are not obeyed as law. This history of aggression may manifest itself as cruelty to animals or children. And above all else, he blames others for his behavior. There is no inner growth. No self-reflection. Just a pure, raw, unhinged desire for violence.

We all get angry. But domestic abuse perpetrators take it to a whole new level. They have anger issues. Uncontrolled and unmanaged rage frequently produces abusive behavior. The source of this anger varies, but it is usually tied to some sort of past traumatic event. Unresolved trauma sparks anger when triggered by a person, circumstance, or place. Because this anger comes out of nowhere, it's that much harder to control when it manifests itself abusively.

Some abusers cite growing up with an addict as a reason for their problems. An addict blames others as to why they engage in their own self-destructive behavior. While the victims are often forced to remain silent and accept whatever insults or punches are hurled their way, the end result is a lot of pent-up anger. As an adult, a child who grew up around addictions subconsciously seeks out others to blame for their trauma.

This is why so many men have control issues…because their own lives spiraled out of control. Ironic, isn't it? Sure, some people like to be in charge. It just naturally occurs to them. But for abusers, being in the driver's seat 24/7 serves a much darker purpose. In an effort to gain or remain in control of others, they utilize inefficient means of dominance, such as bullying or intimidation. While forced control can be quickly executed, it does not have lasting qualities. True leadership is void of abusive techniques. Any man who needs to physically assault a woman in order to show that he's "the boss" has much bigger problems.

Rather than share power and responsibility, abusers fail to understand peaceful coexistence. They mistake boundaries for personal attacks on their character or ability to lead. Abusive people tend to lack the understanding of where they end and another person begins. They see their spouse/child/friend as an extension of themselves and, therefore, that person is not entitled to have any boundaries. The lack of distance means a person is subject to whatever the abuser decides. For a woman, it's a terrifying way to live. Like walking on eggshells…forever.

And despite the show of bravado, men who abuse really are afraid. People who do and say things out of fear tend to use their emotions as justification for why another person needs to do what is demanded. It's as if the fear is so important or powerful that nothing else matters except what is needed to subdue it. What's easier? Tackling the fear that you will always be under crushing financial debt, or swearing at your wife because she forgot to change the batteries in a clock? Of course, the latter! Rather than face his own fears, an abusive man puts his focus elsewhere, like mentally beating up his partner over nonsense.

Stripped away of excuses, at the end of the day, we know that abusers lack empathy.

It is far easier to abuse others when there is no empathy for how the victim might feel. Some types of head trauma, personality disorders, and environmental traumas can cause a person to lack the ability to express empathy, but if it's ongoing and the abuser refuses to seek treatment, or therapy, then this becomes a choice. They might have a personality disorder. Though just because a person is diagnosed with a personality disorder does not mean that they will be abusive. However, the lack of an accurate perception of reality greatly contributes to abusive behavior. If a person is unable to see their behavior as abusive, then they will keep doing it. Hence why they never change! Nobody forces them to.

When a person reaches the end of their rope, it is not uncommon for them to lash out at whoever is conveniently close. Think of it as a mental breakdown, where all the things stuffed inside come pouring out in a destructive, rather than constructive, manner. And women are easy targets.

They become the punching bags – literally. Men who abuse might claim that they are "exhausted" with life's struggles and then employ defense mechanisms such as denial, projection, regression, and suppression. These are utilized when a person is backed into a corner. Instead of taking space, they come out swinging and retaliate in an abusive manner. None of it is acceptable.

And yet, women who have died from domestic abuse have been getting buried for centuries.

Chapter Eleven

Regret

Here's a muddy question: do abuser's feel guilt and shame? Or do they truly not have a shred of remorse for the awful things they've done?

The unfortunate answer is…no. The majority of abusers do not regret what they did. Yes, it is painful to hear that, but the majority of abusers do not regret their actions. This is because they lack self-awareness and the empathy required to understand the hurt, psychological damage, and suffering they have caused. Abuse is often seen as how they deal with corruption. It doesn't seem like a big deal. By justifying or minimizing their treatment of others, they blame the victim. If they regretted it, they would openly admit that it was their fault. Yet, they never do. They blame the victim because they need to see themselves as a good man in power - even if they are abusive. This is usually the only way to ensure that their victims stay with them, as abusers have low self-esteem.

Because the abuser thinks that he is doing right by his victim, he doesn't feel any guilt or shame. There's no regretting it. A person who honestly regrets their shameful acts feels sorry and immediately apologize to their partner because they know they did wrong by acting out in anger. Nobody is perfect, after all. We all do and say things we later regret. The problem lies in the fact that abusers feel no repentance because they don't believe they did anything wrong in the first place!

On the rare occasion that an abuser actually apologizes genuinely for his actions, what then? Only time will tell. Did he really stop? Or does the abuse continue to creep in? It starts in small ways. A rude comment here. A not-so-gentle push there.

In Love With A Monster
Life in an Abusive Relationship

Until finally, another volcanic eruption happens that sends the victim right back into the pit of abuse.

Consider this case. A man named John is an abuser. He always abuses his wife. If she does anything wrong, even a tiny thing, he gets angry very quickly and calls her "stupid," "an idiot," or "a useless woman." But later, he comes to the realization that, actually, his wife did not make a mistake at all! Perhaps he misread the situation. Still, the damage is done. Once he abused his partner, he never offered an apology or said, "Honey, I'm sorry. Please forgive me." Why? Because even though the mistake was never hers to begin with, the abuser doesn't regret his words. Without any concrete consequences to generate empathy, abusers rarely feel emotions that do not directly serve their own selfish agenda.

For a victim who has either experienced abuse firsthand or witnessed a loved one go through the horrors, the memories never truly fade away...

I remember when I finally did my best. He rolled his eyes, promised that he would change, just like he did last time. But I knew, deep down in my heart, that it would not change. Rather, he just really wanted to see me. He hit me, he verbally assaulted me, and he cheated on me. He was, and still is, a terrible man. As bad as he was, I often wanted to know if he felt any remorse for hurting someone so badly. I wasn't going to ask him because I couldn't tell if he was ever telling the truth. So, I decided to go online to find out if abusers felt remorse when their loved ones are hurt.

And much to my disappointment, my worst fears were confirmed. Domestic abusers may feel regret, but not for their victims…only for themselves when they are finally held accountable for their heinous crimes.

The story sounds incredible, right? Almost unbelievable. Well, you have to understand something about abusers. They are not happy people. These individuals are miserable, and they know that they are monsters. Their inferiority complexes are so bad, so overwhelmingly toxic, that they must have complete control over others who they perceive as weak in order to feel better about themselves. So, as long as the means justify the ends (in their minds), regret will *never* be an option.

Sustaining abuse is the endgame. The goal is to keep the wheel spinning endlessly. While we know that there is no logical justification for abuse to take place, in any form, abusers have convinced themselves that the whole reason why they abuse…is for control. It's their style. By extension, they also believe it is their inherent right. Abusing others is a way of being in charge of something in their life. In exchange for making somebody else feel insecure, they gain power. The cost of another's life is a price

In Love With A Monster
Life in an Abusive Relationship

they are willing to pay, gladly! They are denying who the real devil is. Calling out the abhorrent actions is a wasted effort. Domestic abusers will deny any wrongdoing on their part until they are blue in the face, because being abusive isn't just an unsavory character trait. No, for them, it's about survival of the fittest. Abuse is a way of life. Like a shark or other top predator in the animal kingdom, they are incapable of compassion.

In many cases, abusers only regret their actions once they are forced to see the consequences pointed out by a higher authority figure. A victim, her children, family members, concerned neighbors, and friends could all raise questions about the abuser's deeds, but nothing changes. Not until a third party shows up who refuses to cave into the abuser's denial.

Oftentimes, it's not until a police officer places a man under arrest, or a judge orders a restraining order, that an abuser finally has his first inkling of regretful feelings. For many abusers, this overwhelmingly seems to be the case. But by then, the damage is done. All that's left to do is hold the abuser accountable in whatever small ways we can. That's why exposing their actions in public is so key. The longer abuse hides in the shadows, the more violent it gets. It shouldn't take yellow tape around a crime scene for people to wake up to the deadly realities of domestic abuse.

In Love With A Monster
Life in an Abusive Relationship

For psychopaths, narcissists, and socialists, the day of reckoning hits when their toy has been taken away. Like a toddler throwing a temper tantrum, he'll scream and whine. How dare a woman question his way of doing things? How dare she speak up? Oh, sure, he's angry. But only because he regrets that his game has been paused. Not because he hurt anyone. The rage is misplaced. It's not genuine regret or anger…it's the fear of being exposed for the disgrace he is. When people hurt others repeatedly, they don't care about any physical harm or mental health issues they may be causing their victims.

Actually, abusers enjoy it. This harm keeps their victims meek and afraid. Occasionally, a well-intentioned person might try to understand the perspective of an abusive man. For those who are sympathetic to abusers, being forced to confront their issues and seeing the consequences can occasionally lead to real remorse – assuming they are not in denial. However, it goes without saying, most abusers simply don't care enough to change their ways.

How could someone be so cruel? On purpose? It boggles the mind. And yet, we know that abusers are deranged individuals. An abuser creates a host of misconceptions to get his partner to doubt herself and make it possible for him to lead her down dead-end paths. Promises of never-ending care. A life of luxury. Love-bombing tactics. These are the lures a domestic abuser uses to entrap his victims in a web of lies. Once she sees how sticky the situation has become, it's nearly impossible to break free.

Okay. So, we have dispelled those dark myths about whether or not abusers feel regret (recap, they don't!). We can now zero in on the roots of what's known as "steamrolling styles of abuse." You will likely recognize a bunch of them. As you read through the following examples, try to imagine how difficult it would be to separate fact from fiction if you were caught in a cycle of domestic abuse. This process isn't for the faint of heart! But it's necessary if we are to peek behind the curtain and see just how evil the issue of domestic abuse really is.

An intimate relationship involves a steady flow of decisions to be made every single day. In a marriage, for instance, there are conflicting basic needs to negotiate, schedules to work around, and desires to balance. Daily questions arise, such as: who is going to clean up the mess in the kitchen? How much time should we spend alone together, and how much with other friends? Where do our other hobbies and interests fit into our priorities? How will we process and resolve annoyances or hurt feelings? What rules will we have for our future or current children?

The mindset that an abuser brings to these choices and tensions can make him impossible to get along with because, once again, he's at the wheel. Abusive men typically are convinced that control of the household – and by extension, a woman – belongs to him, and him alone. This makes having meaningful conversations with abusers almost impossible.

Look at this example. Let's call our guy "Kyle." Kyle is a naturally abusive person. He always remains angry. Thus, his wife is terrified of him. He gets heated very quickly and abuses her. After a long day at work, he acts deranged. Even if she tries to do something stress-free with him, he doesn't recognize it and thinks his wife is in the wrong. No matter what she does, it's never quite good enough or up to Kyle's standards. Why? Simple. Because Kyle loves the feeling of power he gets when he steamrolls all over his wife's goodwill and autonomy.

Interestingly, for some abusers, it may take years to begin to figure out that they are acting this way. Abuse is so ingrained in their psyche that many men don't even realize it; they are clueless to how horrible they really are. That's why they never feel bad when someone lives with them and puts up with their behavior. If the word "sorry" eventually gets said, it often comes years upon years later. It is because their mental level is not at an evolved stage in which they can rationally control their anger so, instead, they weaponize their rage and use it to abuse their partner.

In Love With A Monster
Life in an Abusive Relationship

Here's another scenario. We will call this man Eric. Just like Kyle, Eric is an abusive person. He always gets angry at little things, like accidently leaving a window open or not adding his favorite ingredient to a meal. As a result, he verbally abuses his girlfriend, Sarah, by calling her stupid and lazy. This happens randomly at first. Yet, over time, the occurrence builds up until the verbal accusations are taking place at least twice per day. But Eric's girlfriend loves him. Sarah believes that he will change and stop abusing her. "Maybe it was his upbringing," she guesses. "Perhaps, with love and patience, I can teach him." This could be true, but research tells us that in a yearning to understand Eric, the girlfriend is risking her own mental health and safety. If the abusers wanted to, they could try to stop themselves from hurting others whenever they wanted.

Seriously, it doesn't take much to pick up a phone and ask for help! Do they? Of course not. The reason why domestic abusers don't seek help outside of the relationship is because they honestly don't care about their victims. They are master narcissists. They care only about their own wants and needs, always.

No matter what situation Sarah finds herself in, the best option at that point is for her and her abuser to break up. Eric obviously sees no reason to change. By staying with Eric and holding onto the belief that it will get better, Sarah is not preventing the abuse from happening again. Actually, the opposite! She is more likely to add to it because her abuser knows, without a doubt, that he will continue to get away with his malicious actions. Like puppies, they have both been trained. Eric, to be abusive without consequences. And Sarah, to accept the abuse. At the end of the day, victims can't change abusers – nor should they be asked to. Some therapists say, "If you love your abuser, you will let them go and give them space for different things." But more importantly, if you love yourself, you will do what you can to quit, instead of maintaining a toxic relationship.

And really, it's not any woman's responsibility to "fix" a broken man. As hard as it is to accept this when it's happening to someone we love, a victim of domestic abuse must walk away. The alternative is to waste a lifetime waiting for a monster to suddenly have an epiphany and wake up and understand what it means to truly love and be a decent human being. This will never, never, never happen. The unhappiness victims feel is nothing compared to the joyous freedom they report once they finally leave.

Torment or freedom? The choice is ours.

Chapter Twelve

Guilt & Victim Blaming

Abusers see themselves as heroes. Crazy, right? They often accuse their victims of committing unforgivable crimes because they themselves are guilty. That's why microscopic problems in a relationship with an abuser usually balloon into gigantic fights and arguments. An abusive man will say anything to deflect the negative attention off of himself, even if it's something as stupid as yelling about a misplaced television remote or too long of a phone call.

In their version of reality, they *are* the hero. They're the ones holding the household together. They are in charge of the narrative. Question any of this, and a woman is in for a world of trouble. This is normally the main way they are able to live with themselves and their actions, since abusers have historically low confidence. They cling to the fantasy where they are the protagonists.

It's frequently said that abusers are only genuinely sorry once their partner leaves them, when they get captured for their conduct, or when their activities are caught in the disapproving gaze of the public eye. This is their sad reality. Hence, why they prefer to maintain a fictional life about themselves in their minds. For maniacs, narcissists, and sociopaths, this is the point we mentioned before, when their toy has been removed. The game is over. And so, they fly into a rage! They are vexed. Furious that their sinful plot has been uncovered (not that they hurt anybody). Individuals who are classified as abusers, mixed with anarchistic or sociopathic tendencies, couldn't care less about the damage they cause. Actually, they enjoy it.

Here's the truly weird thing about domestic abusers that a great many people don't understand: they regularly refuse to see just how horrendous they are until sometime later. That's the reason why they never apologize in the heat of the moment. They only feel regretful emotions *after* their partner has left. Conciliatory sentiments – if, that's a *big* if, – they ever show up, only do so long after the abuse ends.

Guess what? It's not just abusive men who inhabit a fantasy world. For female victims, their own minds can play tricks on them. When faced with the horrors of being harmed by the one who supposedly loves you, the brain sometimes kicks into a sort of survival instinct. Victims of abuse might try to rationalize why they are being treated so poorly. "Did I do something to deserve this?" is a common phrase we hear from survivors. In one case, scientists found that women who had left, or were in the process of seeking help to escape their abusive relationships, reported overwhelming feelings of guilt. This differed to various degrees. Thanks to the oppressive dynamics of the toxic relationships, guilt manifested itself and wreaked havoc on victims' sense of self-confidence, for example.

Likewise, guilt was used to trick victims into performing sexual acts that undermined their own comfort and safety. In the privacy of the home, many women talk of being abused sexually and allowing this to happen because they felt they somehow "owed" their abuser. As if this isn't horrible enough, the guilt continued to have additional impacts on the victims over time. Guilt is like a seed. Once planted and watered with hatred and neglect, it grows. Survivors have said that one of the main reasons why they stayed for so long was because they would have felt guilty for leaving. It can be embarrassing to get a handle on how bad the situation has gotten, talk openly, or look for help when guilt keeps you feeling like the whole problem rests squarely on your shoulders, not his.

Time after time, we see how women blame themselves. Those who are on the receiving end of violence sometimes believe that they are somehow responsible for their own victimization. They think they deserve to be degraded. Women (and those who are abused in general) who think this way often struggle to leave bad relationships because they have been convinced that their self-worth is directly tied to their bond with the abuser. Rather than be an independent entity, they are connected to the person harming them. This makes it almost impossible to break free.

Take the case of "Jillian" and "Brett." After moving across the country to join her boyfriend, Jillian starts to notice that she is arguing more with Brett. She spent all of her savings on a flight and has yet to find a new job, and so, she is financially dependent on him. In addition, she is a stranger to her new town and is finding it difficult to make friends, spending all of her time with Brett instead. This is the source of their arguments.

One evening, following a bad blowup, Brett pushes Jillian hard enough that she falls down. The next day, she wakes up to bruises on her legs and arms. When she raises the issue with Brett and says what he did was unacceptable, he blames her for disrupting his lifestyle and calls her, "entitled" and "boring." Jillian starts to wonder...*is this true? Am I really asking too much?* Her self-confidence and individuality plummet. Soon, Jillian's world shrinks. All she has left (in her mind) is Brett. At this point, she has become so connected to him that breaking up/leaving feels like an unbearable task. So, she apologizes. The violent event is overlooked, the abuse normalized, and the relationship gets more and more toxic as time goes on.

Psychological abuse, debasements, putdowns, etc., all lead to feelings of shame. Survivors are ashamed about the horrendous individuals they accepted into their lives. What's more important, any effort to voice their concerns is instantly met with further mental torment. This isn't a coincidence! It's calculated on the part of the abuser. He knows that if he dismisses a woman's concerns and makes certain topics untouchable or "off the table," then they will never have to talk about the facts transparently. Therefore, he can go on living in his merry little fantasy world. All the while, the woman suffers in silence.

We know, however, that the guilt is a lie...smoke and mirrors designed to disorient and trick.

Consider the following story. Once upon a time, a close friend reached out to me. She recounted her tale of how, after many failed attempts, she finally succeeded in dumping a harsh ex-boyfriend. The man bawled his eyes out. He promised that he would change, do better, improve as a partner, the works. But she'd heard it all before. He did the same thing last time, and the time before, and she wasn't having it. She knew where it counted, deep down in her heart, that he would never commit to fully changing and be the loving and kind person she needed. Still, the temptation was there.

"Maybe," she said to herself. "Just maybe, he truly *can* see the advantage of being together. Perhaps, this time will be different."

It wasn't. He hit her. Verbally criticized her, and constantly undermined her dreams and ambitions. He was (and still is) an awful individual. As terrible as he seemed to be, she kept going back because she needed to know if he ever felt truly sorry for hurting her so badly. The possibility of change was right there! Why couldn't he do it? She wasn't going to ask him outright if he regretted his actions, since he refused to ever really have full conversations about the issues. Besides, he never took the issue of violence as seriously as she did. Everything had an excuse. She couldn't ask him about it all, since he would never come clean anyways. But still, she wondered...do abusers who claim to love their victims feel any regret...ever?

In search of the answer, she went online. The following is what she found. It was hard to hear, but as we confirmed already, the overwhelming majority of domestic abusers do not hold feelings of remorse for their victims. This woman's research told her that, in fact, abusers fall short on mindfulness and compassion in every way, and so, they lack the ability to understand the torment they have caused their "loved ones."

Suddenly, everything made sense! In her desire to be the glue of the relationship and hold it all together, despite her own suffering, this woman supported the behavior of her abuser because she wasn't able to shift the fault onto the person in question...her ex. To him, every negative comment was in his words, "No biggie." On the off-chance he felt sorry, the ex-boyfriend still managed to shovel most of the blame onto his girlfriend. Tragically, she fell for these lies for years before finally reaching out for help.

The damage was done. Not just from the bruises on her arms and neck, but also to her psyche. Women who fall victim to domestic abuse regularly report long-term mental health issues. Can we blame them?

Of course not. Through ongoing victimization, abusers cause lasting mental harm. Either the abusers do not realize that what they are doing is wrong, or they cannot stop themselves. This piece of information ultimately doesn't matter in the slightest, but it's worth mentioning because, as we know, an abuser will stop at nothing to justify why they did what they did. Sure, an abusive man might blame substance abuse problems or brain damage. Heck, they might even temporarily overcome their abusive tendencies! However, if an individual is willfully abusive and just doesn't care, no number of pleas for reason and compassion will stop him.

It's not a woman's job to prevent her own abuse. To argue that women must step into this role to end a crime committed against them – based purely on gender, remember – is a repulsive form of victim-blaming. Part of the problem is that nobody talks about what abuse is and what it isn't. So long as domestic abuse hides in the dark, we will never be successful in eradicating it.

Really, all most girls learn is that abuse happens when another person purposely hurts us. It can take many forms, from insulting someone to hurting someone physically or mentally. Most abusers are taking advantage of a special relationship, like a

In Love With A Monster
Life in an Abusive Relationship

mother, sister, daughter, grandmother, girlfriend, or wife. On the other hand, men who are caught abusing are rarely held accountable. Society simply shrugs its shoulders and parrots the same old meek advice: seek immediate professional help to deal with your anger issues, substance abuse issues, poor parental abilities or poor boundaries, and personal relationship strategies. Is there any follow up? Accountability? Legal repercussions? One-on-one support for the female in the relationship? Nope. A meeting here, a therapy session there, and domestic abusers have full ability to carry on (or not) as they see fit.

As a result, the victimization bleeds into others. As lines and boundaries get crossed, as the abuse worsens, and as the abusive man becomes more powerful, any children in the household begin to, sadly, feel the effects of living with an abusive parent. We know that there are many types of child abuse, including neglect, physical abuse, sexual exploitation, and emotional abuse.

In some communities, physical discipline by parents who do not seriously harm or scar a child is not considered abuse. Though, any child psychologist will argue that physical discipline is definitely a form of abuse. Ask a child, and they most certainly would agree. Plus, there are literally hundreds of alternatives of non-violence available. So, why on earth do so many men instantly turn to physical abuse as a means of communication?

To answer this tricky question, let's look at some examples. First, we will visit Mr. "X." He's a married man. He has two children who are school-aged kids in grades 2 and 7. They spend all their time playing video games or are on their phones. Mr. "X" often grows angry at the way the children fight and bicker loudly over who can play which game and when. So, he physically abuses them with slaps and whacks in order to get them to stop playing video games constantly. "Excessive use of screens may harm your eyesight!" he thunders. When his wife asks him to speak more calmly to the kids, he then turns and roars at her. As we can clearly see, Mr. "X" justifies this kind of abuse because he says it is only for the betterment and health of his children.

What Mr. "X" doesn't realize, however, is that emotional abuse can lead to neurological disorders. A child's brain is still developing until the late teens. It's not a shock that being raised in an abusive environment can have long and profound effects on the human brain.

Children are innocent. They easily believe everyone. The effects of emotional abuse can be traumatic and devastating, both short-term and long-term. Survivors (both young and old) often suffer from low self-esteem, anxiety, depression, and feelings of helplessness. Many people face deep embarrassment, guilt, and self-loathing because these are feelings that the abuser has deliberately cultivated in them, and it is the result of mistrust and misunderstanding that lead to abusive relationships. Often, shame and guilt force children to remain silent about their experiences and can act as a barrier for a mother to leave a bad relationship.

Even if a victim is already away from the relationship, the psychological pain can be overwhelming, shaping their understanding of themself and the world around them. This is especially true in the absence of a strong social support network, which abusers often cut off from them to increase their dependence. To an abuser, children are the perfect targets. They're naïve, powerless, and lack the words and worldly experience to know just how twisted the violence truly is. That's why so many children confuse abuse for love. They don't know any better.

For some people, emotional abuse can then lead to worsening neurological disorders. Although there is no clinical definition of this phenomenon, it generally refers to the point at which psychological distress affects daily functioning. This loss of function occurs when the effects of emotional abuse become more severe. Dr. Philip Thames describes a common finding.

In Love With A Monster
Life in an Abusive Relationship

He says that the exact characteristics of a neurological disorder may vary from person to person, but it is also common to participate in social and professional activities, as well as lack of reduced self-care (including food and personal hygiene). In addition to feelings of depression and anxiety, a victim of domestic abuse may experience sleep disturbances, medication, delusions, obsessive thoughts, and physical symptoms such as gastrointestinal upset, tremors, and muscle tension. Terrible, right? Emotional abuse can be so bad, it actually alters our bodily structure!

Sometimes, the most annoying symptoms are not found in the presence of extreme anxiety, but in their absence – as in, a woman stops feeling anything at all. She becomes cold. Remote. Mentally shut down and void of emotions on either end of the spectrum, both happy and sad. Nervous disorders do not occur when you are in a healthy relationship. Survivors often report experiencing freedom from nervous breakdown only *after* the relationship has ended, sometimes even years later. This is especially true if a victim never got a chance to carry out her normal life experiences in a healthy way. Learning to live free from the abuse you are so used to enduring creates almost a Stockholm-like syndrome; thrilled to be rid of the monster, but oddly, missing the familiarity of the cage he kept you in....

Chapter Thirteen

Mental Health Issues Do Not Equal Abuse

Interestingly, research has suggested that emotional abuse may play a role in the development of chronic conditions such as fibromyalgia and chronic fatigue syndrome.

In Love With A Monster
Life in an Abusive Relationship

Also, a person can experience insomnia, chronic pain, social nervousness or fear of isolation, guilt, anxiety, etc. To illustrate this point, let's examine Alice. She's dating a guy, and they have a pretty strong relationship. But her boyfriend is not loyal to her. He's a cheater. He has slept around with many other girls. Also, he begins using Alice only to fulfill his sexual desires, and after the deed is done, immediately starts ignoring her.

In addition, Alice's boyfriend emotionally abuses her, calling her crazy for always assuming the worst and telling all his friends that she is paranoid. Alice begins to question herself. *Am I really making things up? Are these all just wild assumptions I have about him? Should I ignore the warning signs and pretend like everything is fine because maybe, one day, he'll stop?* This takes a huge toll on Alice's mental health. Soon, this anxiety seriously affects her at work as well as at home. Three months later, her doctor diagnoses her with a neurological disorder.

At domestic abuse hotlines, stories like these come through all the time. One typical experience is that abuse is brought about by a male partner's own mental health struggles with bipolar disorder, melancholy, tensions, posttraumatic stress disorder, being raised to be a narcissist, or having a very shy character. While these are legitimate psychological health conditions, they don't directly cause abuse. Nothing in the Diagnostic and Statistical Manual of

In Love With A Monster
Life in an Abusive Relationship

Mental Disorders, fifth version (DSM-5), expresses that a psychological disorder exclusively makes a partner act out abusively in a relationship. Still, be that as it may, there are a few designations that raise the alert level to future dangers of becoming abusive. If a man suffers from a psychological sickness, this will generally affect all zones of his life.

For example, troubles at work, collaborations with companions or coworkers, family commitments, and individual relationships such as friendships. As seedy as domestic abuse is, there's never a guarantee that it will be hidden forever. Eventually, at some point, an abusive man will slip up. It's then that the mask falls off and, suddenly, those around him see his true ugly face. Basically, a man's relationship with a woman isn't all that different from his relationships in the outside world. Abusive behavior conducted in a private partner relationship will always be exposed. It's just a matter of when, and to whom. One thing's for sure! Being psychologically ill doesn't make you more likely to abuse. But if you do choose to act abusively, everyone is going to find out sooner or later.

Of course, that doesn't stop some men. Since abusive practices typically happen in one's cozy home life, an abusive partner won't show their negative or hurtful practices with companions, coworkers, or relatives if they can help it. Hiding their wrongdoing is so much easier! And hide it they do. An abusive partner will, in general, put on what can be viewed as a "phony cover" for the remainder of the world to see. At the point when it's simply the victim and the abusive partner together, that veil falls off, and the victim sees an alternate side that others aren't allowed to see. This is what we previously referred to as "the mask." The gigantic problem with this is that the effect of being the only person who is privy to the abusive behavior is also most often the victim herself! She frequently feels that nobody will believe her if she speaks up, since nobody else has seen the abusive practices.

There's a lack of trust. This additionally makes it simpler for the abusive individual to cause their partner to feel liable for their abusive conduct, which strengthens the detachment overall. To everyone else, her partner is a peaceful shepherd. But deep down, he's really just a wolf in sheep's clothing.

Lundy Bancroft, creator of *Why Does He Do That?* (2002), explains that an abusive partner's "esteem framework is unfortunate, not their brain research." Indeed, it can seem like an abusive partner has a psychological instability when they get furious and utilize physical or boisterous attacks. On the off-chance that the abusive treatment was brought about by psychological instability, the partner would likewise shout at, as well as hit, their relatives, companions, and colleagues when vexed. But obviously, he doesn't! With domestic abuse, children nevertheless, the abuser, as a general rule, shouts at *only* his partner. So, we see how his nature might leak a little outside of the home, but typically, on the same scale as within it. The nastiest of abuse he saves just for his wife/girlfriend.

To be fair, abuse and dysfunctional behavior can occur. There are lots of instances of people who have psychological issues and are abusive to their partners. There are also numerous people who exhibit dysfunctional behavior and are sound and steady partners! In the event that your partner has a dysfunctional behavior and is abusive towards you, it's imperative to remember that the psychological instability and abusive practices should be tended to independently by the abusive partner. Let's repeat: they *are* separate issues. It is the abusive partner's obligation to search for help and make their own arrangement for dealing with their psychological instability and be responsible for their abusive behavior.

And on the likely chance that a partner *isn't* taking ownership of his activities, *isn't* admitting to the amount they're harming you, and *isn't* searching for proficient assistance, well, then, at that point, this is a glaringly obvious indication that your partner isn't eager to change! In the event that this is the situation, the abuse in the relationship will proceed and rise after some time. Get out. Pack a bag. Leave. Because the stats show, it's only going to get worse.

In Love With A Monster
Life in an Abusive Relationship

Women are often lulled into a fantasy with their new beau. He seems so sweet. So good-natured and gentle. When the demon finally erupts, the experience can be quite shocking. We ask ourselves, was this a one-time occurrence? It can be extremely difficult to wade through the confusion and fear. The accompanying inquiries may help explain whether what your partner is doing is real abuse or a symptom of some bigger psychological issue.

A woman dealing with the first red flags should ask herself: *Does my partner holler or shout at others (companions, coworkers, and relatives) outside of our relationship? Does my partner make others check in to see where they're at and who they're with? Does my partner hit others outside of our relationship? Does my partner limit the speech of or verbally tear down others? Does my partner compel others to do things that they disapprove of? Does my partner make dangerous threats to others when they state something my partner doesn't agree with?*

Ideally, a woman will laugh these questions off. How absurd! No, no, and very much no, should be the answers to each and every statement. But on the off-chance that she answered "yes" to the greater portion of the inquiries, at that point, there is no doubt that the male partner is abusive without psychological disorders coming into play. A majority of "yes" answers indicate that it's conceivable that a partner is well on his way to being very abusive, and furthermore, might be encountering some type of emotional wellness issue or disease on the side. Lundy Bancroft's celebrated book, *Should I Stay or Should I Go?* has a section on untangling a partner's emotional well-being issues from abusive practices. She tells us that associating with a supportive group of people, including a fellow domestic violence survivors or guides who have practical experience in domestic violence, may help bolster you in making the right choices regarding how to safely exit the relationship…quickly.

But regardless of whether a woman's partner has a psychological issue or not, there will never, ever, ever be a good excuse for abuse! We are adamant that abuse is a decision somebody makes so as to keep up force and exert authority over a partner. In the event that a partner is abusive towards you, whether or not they have a diagnosable illness, they still have no right to treat you like garbage. A woman should always have the right be in a cherished, steady, trusting, and safe relationship 100% of the time, even if she herself fails to realize that.

Chapter Fourteen

Why Victims Stay & How They Get Trapped

An infuriating conundrum: Why do people stay in abusive relationships? Here's the thing, abusive relationships are very complex situations, and it takes a lot of courage to let go. Abuse is about power and control. When a survivor leaves her vile relationship, she threatens the abuser with unwanted change. Abruptly, everything has changed! Who is this woman with a voice and mind of her own? How dare she plot to run away?

When a woman decides, once and for all, that she is completely and totally done, and that the relationship is over, her actions might cause her partner to retaliate in harmful ways. As a result, survivors of abuse report that leaving is often the most dangerous thing. There are physical dangers, like assault. Beyond that, there's also the risk of losing important assets that are key to survival, like access to a shared bank account or insurance on a family vehicle. A frozen bank account isn't exactly conducive to starting a new life of freedom, huh?

Beyond the physical dangers of fleeing the abusive situation, there are countless other reasons why people might choose to *stay* in their relationships. No matter what the circumstances are, survivors are entitled to cooperate in decision-making and be empowered to regain control of their lives! But that doesn't mean leaving is easy. Common reasons for wanting to stay in an abusive relationship include fear, threats, lack of resources, shame, having a disability, cultural upbringing, immigration status worries, or because of children.

First up, fear. Let's face it, abuse is scary. If a person decides to leave their relationship because of concerns about their partner's actions or their ability to be independent, they will probably be afraid of the consequences. A victim often feels that if she tries to leave her abusive boyfriend or husband, then the abuser will kill her. This isn't an exaggeration, unfortunately. Literally hundreds of women are murdered as a result of domestic violence every year, and many of them were killed as they were in the process of escaping.

Here's a situational example to think about. Nicole is living in an abusive household. Her husband always shouts at her, and they just had a baby together. Nicole hoped that their new infant would cool his temper, but in actuality, things just got more violent. One day, Nicole witnesses her husband scream at the baby because he is "sick and tired of listening to it cry!" Nicole decides this is no longer a safe situation for either herself nor her child, and she must leave. But she's terrified at the prospect because she attempted to leave once before when they were newly married, and her husband threatened to kill her for even thinking about it.

Likewise, abuse is cyclical. If someone has grown up in an environment where abuse was common, they may not know what a healthy relationship looks like. As a result, they may not be skilled enough to distinguish between whether their partner's behavior is healthy or unhealthy. Take Bob, for instance. It is a habit of Bob's to act very sweet and loving one second, and then do a complete 180 degree turn as he becomes enraged and cruel. His wife, Rebecca, was raised by a father who acted in a similar way towards her mother. This carried on for over forty years. Now, Rebecca can't recognize whether Bob is in a good mood or bad. She doesn't know what to do about her husband's behavior, or even if it's something to be concerned about, because, to her, it feels normal.

Shame, shame, shame! It's an insidious feeling that eats away at the soul. And yet, acknowledging and admitting that you have been abused can be difficult. A survivor may feel that they have done something wrong, that they deserve to be abused, or that being abused is a sign of personal weakness. We know that blaming is a common tactic some abusers use to stay in control.

Shame can strengthen a victim's sense of responsibility for their partner's abusive behavior. Nobody knows this better than case study, Ms. "L." Her partner liked nothing more than to belittle her. He would shout at Ms. "L" and always bully her, saying things like, "you're an idiot and should be ashamed of how poorly you do x, y, and z. After a few months of hearing this false rhetoric, Ms. "L" thought that it was her fault the marriage was failing. Not her abusive partner's. Saddest of all, the shame she felt kept her from ever speaking publicly about her unhappiness.

Ah, threats. The number three weapon in an abuser's toolkit. Survivors may be intimidated by verbal or physical threats, or by threats to spread information (i.e., revenge posts on social media, pornography, calling a boss/priest/family member to gossip, etc.). This could also include sharing secrets or confidential medical details. For LGBTQ+ people who have not yet come out, threatening a woman can be an opportunity to, once again, exert total control and convince her not to leave, lest the public find out about her secret sexuality preferences before she is ready.

In addition, women sometimes have a lack of resources to trek out on her own.

She may have been financially relying on her partner or have previously been denied a job opportunity, a place to sleep, a language aid, or a network to rely on in times of crisis. These factors can make it impossible for anyone to leave an unpleasant situation. There are plenty of examples of women who said they did not have the financial resources to survive after leaving.

Less talked about, but no less important, is the topic of disability. If a victim of abuse relies on other people for physical/psychological support, she may feel that her well-being is directly linked to her spot in the relationship. Lack of visible alternatives for support if someone has a disability can have a huge impact on someone's decision to leave an abusive relationship.

Housing, income, and access to assistance are three areas that do not get enough attention when investigating domestic abuse cases. Mrs. "O" has firsthand experience. She was healthy before, but after some time, she became physically disabled due to an accident at the factory where she works. Now, she needs the support of her partner to do even basic tasks, like using the bathroom. But in exchange, she has to bear the abusive situation because she knows that, now, she is disabled, and she can't do anything about her husband's excessive violence.

Immigration status is similar. Women who do not have proper documentation may fear that reporting abuse will affect their pending immigration status. If their English proficiency is limited, these concerns can be exacerbated by a confusing and criminal legal system, and their inability to state their case to others. Let's switch genders for a moment and tackle Aryan, as an example. Aryan migrated to the USA from India. He wanted to live in the USA his whole life. He finds a girl who is a US citizen and marries her. But the honeymoon stage ends quickly. She is a very abusive person. She always abuses her husband and threatens that she will divorce him and send him back to his home town if he doesn't do everything exactly as she demands. Now, Aryan feels he has no choice but to accept this abusive relationship and poor living conditions if he wants to stay in the USA.

And it's not just a North American issue. Cultural context matters when talking about domestic abuse. Traditional customs or beliefs can influence a person's decision to live in a horrendous situation, whether it's via pressure from family or the wider community. There are countless cases of women living in abusive relationships and unable to escape, partly because of their cultural upbringing. Take a new bride, for example. During her engagement, she raised concerns about her future husband. He had a history of getting into physical altercations with strangers, and she knew he had bullied his sisters and mother more than once. Still, she marries him. When the physical violence starts up, and she finds herself becoming a victim, she feels that she cannot leave because the cultural norm in her society is to stay with her partner under any circumstances.

We've all heard the wedding vows that say, "For richer and poorer, in sickness and in health." But what about when the person you marry is directly responsible for your ailments? Do you stay? For women living in culturally-oppressive circumstances, the answer can be difficult.

In the example used above, everyone knew this man was abusive beforehand. They just didn't care. Without any pressure to change his ways, he carried

In Love With A Monster
Life in an Abusive Relationship

on beating his new wife. One day, the situation got so frightening that she finally said, "That's it! I'm done." But then a troubling thought occurred. What about the children? Many survivors may feel guilty or responsible for disrupting their family unit. Keeping the family together can not only be a reason why the survivor cannot escape, but can also be used by their partner as a tactic to essentially hold the victim hostage. For women in low-income countries that lack access to shelters and funding aimed directly at rehabilitating survivors of domestic abuse, the choices are slim. Stay, and keep placing yourself and the children at risk? Or leave, and open them up to a whole new world of unknowns? Clearly, there's no easy answer.

As survivors of domestic abuse, our minds get warped. We have been so conditioned to believe that "this is just the way things are" or "maybe it was my fault" or "he can change" that it's not until blood is spilt, or a woman is dead, that we, as a society, finally wake up to the endemic of violence sweeping our communities. Another way that we fail women is by blurring the lines between what is love and what is possessive red flag behavior! Love isn't abuse. Simple as that.

However, experiencing abuse and feeling real love for a partner who is hurting you are not mutually exclusive. Yes, believe it or not, we can love those who hurt us. Survivors still have strong and intimate feelings for their abusive partners. They may have children together, want to maintain their family, or the abuser may be sweet and charming (especially at the beginning of the relationship). There's always a faint glimmer of hope within the survivor that, maybe, their partner will return to normal. Woefully, it's a false promise. No amount of love can fix a broken man. If he is physically and/or psychologically abusive, but says he cares deeply for a woman, that isn't love. That is manipulation at its finest.

Chapter Fifteen

The Barriers to Getting Free

In an abusive relationship, it can be challenging to separate fact from fiction. Distorted thoughts are common. As we have seen, keeping a victim in a constant state of fear is a painful, but effective, tactic abusers use to control and hurt others. This ever-present state of confusion also lends to feelings of confusion, suspicions, paranoia, and even self-blame.

Over time, the insults and harassment wear a person down. Even the strongest woman grows tired of the never-ending abuse. She might feel frustrated or guilty. Others – like the friend I mentioned earlier – deal with it by minimizing the abuse. She used to say, "I stayed because I don't feel like emotional abuse is *really* that bad compared to hitting." Or, when her fiancé would limit her monetary spending on essential items, she would justify it with comments such as, "He's just trying to help us budget better." Because the words didn't leave physical scars on her body, she figured it was okay. The abuse got normalized. It wasn't until the words turned into bloody red cuts and purple bruises that she finally woke up to how poorly she was being treated.

Distressingly, some women, who are victims of abuse, turn to self-harm as a way to cope. As a result of the degrading treatment, self-harm, such as cutting, hair pulling, and a general neglect of overall health and hygiene, becomes a way to take back control of their lives. Survivors in support groups have been quoted saying, "He convinced me that I was useless and lonely" as well as "I felt that I had done something wrong. It felt like I deserved the pain."

In Love With A Monster
Life in an Abusive Relationship

How? This is the question we must ask ourselves. How do we, as a society, put up with such disturbing events being played out right under our noses? Is it fear? Of course, we know that fear is a powerful motivator. Threats of physical and emotional harm are used by men to control and trap women, not only in their homes, but also in their workplaces, among their wider family units, and on the street. Women are much more likely to be victims of gender-based violence than men. All women are raised with this understanding. Even in coffee shops or at the mall, women are not safe from abuse.

Consider these words. "It's dangerous to try and get rid of an abuser." True, no? When trapped in a domestic abuse situation, it quickly descends into a damned if we do, damned if we don't situation. Stay, and the abuse carries on. Attempt to leave, and you might be on the receiving end of threats to hunt you down, kill you, or harm all of your loved ones (including children and pets). It's for these reasons that so many girls, young women, and female victims of domestic abuse never speak up in abusive situations. To voice a concern is in and of itself a very real danger.

How often on social media have you seen men and abusive people hop onto Facebook and Twitter and post a monologue defending their horrendous behaviors? We see it come from celebrities all the time. Comments warp reality, just as they do to a victim's mindset. Look at the rich and famous who have been accused of abuse. We see phrases such as, "I thought I would be a strong man who would never leave her and show her loyalty" and "I will fix it" or "I made a mistake. And I promise to do better." We often hear nothing but excuses, blaming the wrongdoings on past father figures, drug addictions, and religious trauma. But the sad reality is, no woman should need to teach a man how to love. If abuse comes more naturally than compassion and kindness, that is not anyone's job to fix except the individuals themselves.

The end result is always the same. Women cope as best they can. Sacrificing their own safety, they regularly put their children first. "I was afraid he would beat my children if he stopped beating me. And I valued their lives more than my own," is an example from one heartbreaking abuse case. The survivor further explained, "I lived with him for 20 years while I did what I had to do to protect my children, all while I was being abused." Others mentioned similarly misguided (but well-intentioned) reasons for staying. Sometimes, it's for the benefit of their children. "I wanted that for them. Please, be the father our children need," was one desperate plea.

Numerous statements were made about how past experiences with violence distorted their sense of self-worth or understanding about what it means to be engaged in a healthy relationship. Women raised in abusive households talk about how they found someone just like their father or, as one very self-reflective person put it, "Because the animals have raised you, you're in a partnership with the wolves." Still, other survivors mentioned either family or religious pressure. "My mother told me that if I broke up my marriage, God would reject me," confessed one young woman who got married at the tender age of eighteen.

Likewise, finances present a barrier to leaving. Many people referred to financial constraints, and these were often linked to childcare issues. "I had no family, two teenagers, and no money because all of my saving were spent on bills after I suffered a brain injury from a car accident." Other survivors shared how they were unable to retain jobs due to their abusers controlling their movements. Perhaps, most underhand, was the case of a woman named Caroline. She explained how her ex-husband financially deceived her. "My ex made me take out thousands of dollars in my legal name, as a loan. So, I was on the hook. I couldn't leave. The debt was crushing." While physical and verbal assaults are deadly, financial abuse is its own kind of living Hell.

In addition, a common tactic of manipulating partners is to separate their prey from family and friends. Sometimes, it's physical, as one woman explained, "He would discourage me from visiting my parents who lived only 30 minutes away, saying the gas was too expensive, and that it wasted too much time." Other times, loneliness is the emotional manipulation, as one woman was told by her boyfriend, "You can either make new friends, or you can be with me. It's one or the other. You have to choose."

Although these reasons for staying are common, they do not describe every victim and each unique situation. Women can be abusive too, and it's suspected that the numbers of men trapped in abusive relationships is vastly underreported. Regardless of gender, however, it is truly difficult for an outsider to understand what's happening inside a domestic abuse relationship. That's because many victims are reluctant to speak out due to fear and pressure from friends and professionals to "save the marriage" or "work on the relationship." But if more and more people responded to stories of abuse with genuine concern and compassion for victims instead of criticizing, then maybe more victims would finally speak up and get the support they need to live a life free from abuse.

As a society, we need to do better. It's repulsive that women are afraid of societal backlash and fear the repercussions of leaving a domestic abuse situation. For this reason, thousands of women never end their bad relationship or find peace. Instead, they live their whole life with it. The mental health of these women is very poor. Not always, but sometimes, such women are undereducated in ways that would allow them to find their own meaningful independence – like through employment. They also don't necessarily know about women's rights. And get this…even when they are told about their right to live free of violence, the society, as a whole, *still* acts as if such a thing is pure fantasy, is demanding, or unreasonable to expect.

No wonder so many women bury their agony and suffer in silence. Many times, the living conditions also affect any children the couple might have together. Although a woman experiencing domestic abuse does not want the same fate for her daughter, she, nevertheless, may choose to stay as her survival and the child's future depend upon the resources only the male in the relationship can provide.

To paint a clearer picture, let's dig into some case studies. Take Cassie and Glenn, for instance. They have been in a relationship for five years, and at the time of the separation, the couple had between four and five children. They are both Indigenous and have neither been employed recently nor have they received any further training or education. During the relationship, their income was in the form of various welfare benefits. Cassie had been using cannabis regularly since the age of 13, but it was clear soon after the birth of her fifth child that she wanted to ease up on the habit. Glenn is a long-term speed and ice user. His drug addiction increased during this relationship and made him even more violent, especially when he was "coming down" or when he could not easily access drugs. Cassie was abused during her childhood by a family friend, and later, by a close family member, which resulted in her being briefly imprisoned. As an adult, Cassie was also heavily involved in caring for a disabled relative.

Glenn's violence with Cassie began months after the birth of her first child. Glenn hit Cassie on the nose, causing severe pain and bleeding. A passerby called the police, and an ambulance took her to the hospital. A police protection order was issued, allowing Cassie and Glenn to stay together on the condition that Glenn maintains good behavior with Cassie.

At this point, Cassie felt committed to the relationship and hoped that she could influence Glenn to stop his violent ways and drug trafficking. At Cassie's request, Glenn was not charged with assault. Though he never hit the children, he occasionally continued to physically, and later sexually, assault Cassie. She stayed because, with five children and no clear path to employment, she simply didn't know what else to do.

As we can see, getting free isn't easy. While informational flyers, posters, government agencies, and well-meaning individuals make escaping domestic violence sound as simple as deciding to leave, the barriers are high. So are the risks.

Chapter Sixteen

Just Let Her Go

Abusers can have a Jekyll-and-Hyde character. Dr. Jekyll is frequently beguiling and sentimental, may be affectionate, and makes professions of love (recall: love bombing is a favorite trick of the abusers). Women adore Dr. Jekyll and, subsequently, rationalize Mr. Hyde. A woman may not see that the *entire* individual is the issue – she cannot separate the evil from the good. In the event that you have experienced an agonizing relationship with a cruel parent growing up, this is likely the closest comparison on how we can love someone who is bad for us.

Okay, so, here we are. The woman has found her Dr. Jekyll. They get romantically involved. Every now and again, the awful Dr. Hyde pops up for a visit, but generally speaking, things are calm. Then, one day, her boyfriend explodes. He destroys the house, throws away all of his girlfriend's possessions, threatens to murder her…and the police are called. After a lengthy conversation, no charges are filed. The woman – in her state of shock – mentally justifies her abusive outburst. Why?

Well, there are numerous reasons. Firstly, the relationship is still young. Measurements show that victims of violence bear a normal of up to seven assaults. Yes, seven! The predominant explanation is reliance: control by the abuser, embarrassment about her own mistreatment, and a blow to her confidence. Slowly, she begins to hide the abuse by pulling back from loved ones. This causes a snowball effect. Soon, she is filled with even more dread and reliance on her abuser. The abuse itself is experienced as an enthusiastic dismissal with the danger of her own independence being surrendered. Even self-reliant women fall into this trap! This, in turn, triggers feelings of disgrace and fears of more abuse.

Women are often terrified of leaving the person in question, because he has made it feel like an impossible task. A few days after a particularly awful episode takes place, abusive men typically snap right back to their normal selves. It's as if the damage never happened. Survivors describe this feeling as "emotional whiplash." One second, your life is in danger. The next, you are his queen who is smothered in love and affection. Lies, of course. This is done to lure the victim into a deep state of confusion and doubt. Was it really that bad? Did I overreact? Maybe I just misunderstood? Remember, abuse is sneaky. There are always reasons why the individuals love, or once loved, their abusers, frequently with children included in the equation.

To summarize, women stay for the following reasons: they have nowhere else to live, no outside emotional support, childcare concerns, they take the blame for the abuse, denying, minimalizing, and rationalizing the abuse, they still think the abuser loves them, finances, and low self-esteem.

Shame is also a huge indicator of abuse taking place. Victims feel embarrassed. They are mortified, and their confidence has been shattered. Therefore, they conceal the mistreatment from friends and family closest to them, frequently pretending the abuser is a

In Love With A Monster
Life in an Abusive Relationship

"good guy" to hide their own disgrace. And guess what? An abuser couldn't be happier to see this! He will use strategies to build upon this momentum of shame by confining his victim from seeing acquaintances. He'll also offer comments intended to show favoritism or be one-sided. The rules of the abuser's game are simple…either you're for him or against him. There is not an in-between.

On the off-chance that the abuser feels insulted by something you said that slipped out and betrayed his true abusive nature, at that point, a woman needs to agree with his position, or she's in deep trouble. This is intended to exert command over her and solidify her reliance upon her partner. Only his opinion matters. To question it would be disastrous. And so, the abused woman learns to lie, put on a fake mask, pretend to be happy, and conceal the pain.

Why are women afraid to go, even if they've never been hit? It is difficult to give up an illicit relationship for quite a few reasons. There are many motives why one can live with one's partner in an unhealthy or toxic situation. Firstly, society normalizes unhealthy behaviors so that people do not think their relationship is offensive. When you think unhealthy or abusive behavior is normal, it is difficult to identify your relationship as harmful, and so, there is no reason to seek help. In many societies, verbal abuse is considered totally acceptable. The victim feels that verbal abuse is not wrong, so both parties do not feel that their relationship is damaged (even though it most definitely is).

Here's an example. Mr. "V" is living in a town where domestic abuse is normalized. His father yells at his mother daily. And his brother-in-law also speaks rudely to his sister. One afternoon, while in the park having a picnic, Mr. "V" sees his sister crying. "What's the matter?" he asks with concern. She explains that her husband screamed at her moments ago. The whole family saw this happening, but nobody had a problem with it. Mr. "V" doesn't know what to do.

On one hand, he is angry to see his sister upset. But at the same time, men in the town regularly attack their wives, and so, the behavior is normal. In time, the verbal abuse increases to physical abuse. Still, Mr. "V" doesn't interfere. A few years down the road, Mr. "V" gets a phone call informing him that his sister has died. No further details are given. The funeral is planned, her death is mourned, and the family moves on. Yet, there is a little voice inside of Mr. "V's" head that always wonders...should he have stepped in to stop the abuse earlier?

That's an example of physical abuse. Similarly, emotional abuse destroys your self-esteem, making it impossible to hit the refresh button on life. Often, people in emotionally-abusive relationships do not realize that they are being abused because there is no

In Love With A Monster
Life in an Abusive Relationship

obvious violence involved. Also, many people will reject or reduce emotional abuse because they do not think it is as bad as physical abuse. Emotional abuse affects the brain. It literally damages the victim's nervous system. So, to say it isn't as damaging is false! It is equally bad. In some ways, worse.

Have a look at this case. Ryan is an abusive person. He abuses his wife verbally. His favorite names to call her are "pig" and "slob." In time, this affects the mental health of the victim. She loses self-esteem, stops leaving the house, and becomes paranoid about her appearance. After each incident, Ryan half-heartedly apologizes and says he was only joking to be funny.

Often when an abusive situation arises, such as this one, the abuser then does something good or apologizes and promises that they will never do it again. This minimizes the actual misbehavior of their partner. The abuser makes every effort to regain control and keep the victim in the relationship. He can act as if nothing has happened, or he can turn his attention away. This peaceful honeymoon stage can give the victim hope that the abuser has finally changed this time around.

Leaving is dangerous. Like, very dangerous…Many times, leaving an abusive relationship is not only emotionally difficult, but can also be fatal. The most dangerous time in an abusive relationship is post-breakup. Women are 70 times more likely to be killed in the weeks after leaving their abusive partners than at any other time in the relationship. Leaving mentally disturbs both partners. We know of many cases where, once a woman flees, the abuser disappears for a few weeks, only to become so angry, he plots a revenge plan to kill his ex-partner. If this sounds too unimaginable to be true, look up the statistics yourself. It happens. Constantly.

That's because getting away safely is difficult. Not only is planning an escape route a challenge, it is also difficult to escape the control. Abusive men often try to get even with their partners several times before they finally break up. As we previously mentioned, on average, a survivor of domestic abuse will try to quit seven times before she finally leaves for good.

To see how this plays out, we can look at the case of Rachel. She wants out of her boyfriend's apartment because his drug abuse has made him scary to live with. Their walls are filled with holes. He has broken their television. And, in a fit of anger, he pushed Rachel into a closet. Rachel knows that she is in very real danger. She doesn't drive, and she calls her friend to come pick her up for the night. But before the friend can arrive, her boyfriend gets mad one last time. He finds out she is plotting to leave him and refuses to let her go. And so, he kills her.

In Love With A Monster
Life in an Abusive Relationship

Ever heard the term "ride or die?" When pushed to the extreme, this can become literal.

Unhealthy or abusive relationships may linger because one partner wants to stay or reunite after a break as they feel pressured to forgive and forget, or "move on." Pop culture is a symbol of "riding or dying" for your friends and partners, and people make the mistake of literally dying at the hand of their own partner. Sure, loyalty is a great character trait. But a good friend or loving partner will never intentionally hurt you.

Sometimes, a female victim of domestic abuse feels personally responsible for their partner or his behavior. After a conflict, the abuser will turn the situation around and feel guilty, as if there is something wrong with it. This type of behavior is known as *gaslighting*. The abuser feels guilty after some time, and only when his own selfish anger has cooled off does he then apologize to the victim and try to restore their relationship. An example of this is the husband who abuses his partner. After some time when he becomes normal again, he recognizes that he did something wrong. He apologizes to his partner, assuming this cancels out his poor choices. In an effort to "keep the peace," the victim also apologizes, even though she did absolutely nothing wrong. And so, it goes.

In Love With A Monster
Life in an Abusive Relationship

Many people in abusive relationships stay because they love their partner and think things will change. They may also believe that their partner's behavior is due to difficult times, or that they feel like they can change their partner if they are a better partner themselves. But one has to wonder...how much should somebody sacrifice for the sake of another person's growth? To reflect on this question, let's review Mrs. "F," who lives with an emotionally-abusive partner.

Her partner abuses her on little things, but she is still living and is waiting for that day in which the situation will change, and her partner stops abusing her. She tries to be the perfect wife. She is kind, gentle, cooks, cleans, takes care of the kids and their elderly parents, works hard, is affectionate and loving, all to no avail. Finally, one day, she snaps. Mrs. "F" suddenly realizes that, while she was bettering herself to be the most amazing partner possible, her husband was not returning the effort in the slightest. He did not change. There was no reason for him to. Bad behavior cannot be rewarded with good actions. Abusers will not put forth the same energy as their victims. They are narcissist who only take, take, take.

But perhaps, the biggest reason why women can't just let go is this – there is immense social pressure to live in a "perfect relationship." Social media (like Facebook, Instagram, and Twitter) only exacerbate that pressure. Two people in a relationship often find that they feel pressured to show off a perfect fairytale lifestyle; otherwise, society will judge them harshly. This inauthenticity invalidates normal things all couples go through – like minor arguments – and, as a result, add to the toxic nature of a brewing domestic abuse situation.

Not always, but sometimes, a man won't let a woman go because he fears the reactions of others. He knows that if she leaves and tells everyone about how he treated her, then he risks being judged, blamed, sidelined, abandoned, ignored, charged, or kept out of sight. Therefore, he refuses to let her leave. Maybe they live together. Marriage, children, and joint financing are often the main reasons why victims stay.

This dependence is further strengthened in relationships when a partner is empowered in different ways. But there are similar factors that influence young people's decisions to stay in relationships, including mutual friend groups and living conditions. To get away from a domestic abuse situation is to tell the truth. Abusers panic. They know that, if their female partner leaves, they have lost control over the narrative. People will see him for the monster he really is. Consequently, he must set a trap and force her to stay.

In Love With A Monster
Life in an Abusive Relationship

It's a deadly game of cat and mouse. Which is why it is also so frustrating to oftentimes be asked the same question over and over again; why didn't she just go? While there exists an assortment of reasons, it's usually simply that the victim might be secured in a pattern of violence. Earlier, we talked about excuses. Now, we will highlight other basic reasons why victims remain with their batterers. To start, the victim cherishes the abuser and claims he isn't generally vicious.

Likewise, the victim fears her abuser. Dangerous threats are made against the victim, for instance, the abusive man claiming he will execute the victim if the history of his neglect is told to anybody outside the home. Police, in the victim's eyes, offer no guarantee of safety because there are lengthy investigations and court battles that must take place and, unless the victim is willing to press charges, not much can be done in the heat of the moment. Regardless of whether it is a neighbor who reports or not, the abuser may take it out on the victim. Regularly when the police come, the victim won't admit to the beating, even when purple bruises or bloody cuts are obvious. It could very well be that the victim is monetarily reliant on her partner and, not having another source of income, she has no reasonable options to pay for her needs.

Even when the cops do get called, that's just the beginning. Like we discussed previously, social

In Love With A Monster
Life in an Abusive Relationship

expectations are a giant barrier to leaving a bad relationship. Individuals feel they should remain in a relationship and are exceptionally impervious to change, as methods for critical thinking and logic don't always apply in domestic abuse environments. Women regularly report feeling terrified, exhausted, and afraid of what their friends, family, and coworkers will think of them if they admit that the relationship broke down. While there are lots of superficial support for survivors of domestic abuse, on a practical level, the avenues for escape are dismal. Women's shelters are underfunded. Employment offices offer minimum wage jobs. And social support workers are so overworked, they can barely keep their own list of clients straight. This is why many victims feel that it's easier to keep up the fake exterior of a decent marriage.

How do you leave the one person who is your emotional and financial support network? Remember, an abuser will try to pulverize a victim's relationships with friends and family. Being alone means she has limited options. From an abuser's point of view, this is fantastic! Now, she needs him to survive. There's no way she'll be able to leave. Especially if children are involved.

Regularly, the victims remain for the kids "requiring a dad," or out of fear that the abuser may act violently against the kids if the victim attempts to flee. The abuser regularly takes steps to remove the kids from the victim if the victim leaves via a court order. No woman wants to risk losing her children to a psychopath! Thus, she stays.

Even if a judge sides with the victim, there are still concerning legal implications. Just because a courtroom agrees that a man was abusive to his wife/girlfriend doesn't necessarily stop him from retaining his rights as a father. This includes things like visitation rights, access to medical information, the ability to make medical decisions on behalf of his children, and in some states, even the right to full custody if he can prove that, despite the abuse to his partner, he is a fit parent who have never hurt the children.

An abuser will present himself as easygoing and intelligent, minimizing his own wrongdoings in an effort to win over the opinions of others. He does this so that the victim's interests are not paid as much attention to. Disgustingly, this works wonders! Men regularly win shared custody of their children because, in the eyes of the law, they were vicious with only their partner, not their children. That being said, many advocates strongly condemn this legal norm and are working to undo centuries of bias that favor the male parent in domestic abuse cases.

Lastly, a woman might not "just go" because, internally, she has accepted the abuse as being her own fault. A victim might defend the beatings, accepting them as merited. This warped sense of thinking results from being convinced that physical abuse is a part of "discipline." Maybe as a child, a young girl was hit for misbehaving. And so, when her husband acts out violently, the domestic abuse is normalized as a part of everyday life. Though she is a fully functioning adult, the gender imbalance in domestic abuse relationships automatically gives men the power to "dish out discipline" to their wives. Is it deserved? Of course not. Nobody deserves to be hit...ever. And yet, spousal abuse such as this is common in many parts of the world.

The victim on the receiving end might feel guilt or shame, and as a result, she might be reproachful. Oftentimes, survivors report a life of "walking on eggshells." To prevent future violence, they tiptoe around the relationship. Many women who normalize abuse accept that this is simply a way of life, and that they, in some ways, deserve to be treated poorly. False! However, if a woman has been raised to believe that she is the one responsible for her aggressor's actions, it becomes immensely challenging to persuade her otherwise.

Maybe she grew up in a home where one parents beat up the other. In such a circumstance, children learn to consider violence as inescapable. They assume it's normal for men to strike at women, and that all couples must fight in ways that are physically and emotionally abusive. Nothing could be further from the truth, but with so little evidence to the contrary, how would she ever know? Frequently, abused individuals are spurred by pity and sympathy. They get persuaded that the abuse is acceptable, or worse, that it is their job to help the abuser with his "issue" (this might be anger management, drinking, pressure from the outside world, etc.). While helping your partner become a better person is noble, when it comes at the risk of your own well-being – or life – one has to wonder...why are women expected to be therapists for broken men?

Chapter Seventeen

Stockholm or "Prisoner" Syndrome & Likelihood of Murder

Have you ever watched a movie where a kidnapped woman falls in love with her captor? Though it might sound like a fictional scenario, it really does happen! When a hostage starts feeling positive emotions (like admiration, trust, and love) towards their abuser, this psychological response is called *Stockholm Syndrome*. Just like a kidnapped victim, numerous women feel stuck in a "prisoner" bond along these lines with their boyfriend or husband, and this is why they choose to stay in abusive relationships. Since escape feels impossible, survival instincts kick in and convince the brain that, actually, it is safe. However, those who have suffered from Stockholm Syndrome aren't able to completely stamp out the recurring nightmares, confusions, PTSD, and difficulty trusting new people.

Why on earth would a woman develop Stockholm Syndrome? How, we wonder, could any reasonable person fall in love with a monster? Well, we know that abuse typically starts slow. It builds and builds until the victim no longer even recognizes herself, never mind the remnants of her old life. Family and friends are cut off. The ability to move about freely is restricted. The abusive partner becomes the only source of affection in her life, and as a result of her world shrinking so much, a woman in a domestic abuse relationship suddenly begins experience elements of Stockholm Syndrome.

We know that abusers are tricky. What little kindness the abuser does show rarely gets reciprocated. Women who have escaped very bad domestic abuse situations often talk about how they mentally justified the violence by counteracting it

In Love With A Monster
Life in an Abusive Relationship

with an imaginary, made-up illusion of the man they were living with. Even though, deep down, they knew the evil their partner was capable of, they, nevertheless, protected him. Many women explain that they attempted to "get inside the abuser's head," see the world from his point of view, always be happy and cheerful, and deny any wrongdoing in order to maintain the fantasy that everything was okay. After all, they *thought* they were in love! In truth, their minds had been filled with lies.

Those who recover from Stockholm Syndrome face a long road to recovery. In addition to bad dreams, PTSD, overpowering sentiments of dread and uneasiness, trouble thinking clearly, worry in relationships, and a genuine fear for their own security and well-being, survivors also must deal with the challenge of seeing outside specialists. When the one who is supposed to love you turns out to be a villain, it can feel earthshattering. That's why it's so important to cut off the abuser's narrative early on!

Abusive men like to play the hero. They consider themselves defenders with the righteous authority to act however they see fit. They concoct a make-believe world and force their female victims to act the parts assigned, mountainously making sure it's impossible for them to break free or leave. The repercussions are deadly. This is why it's so hard to flee. Once Stockholm Syndrome has taken root, the fantasy feels like reality. Until the abuser is dead or in jail, many women feel like they will never break free.

A life of abuse is no life worth living. And some abusers are life-threatening, anyways! Whether a woman chooses to stay or leave, her life is in danger. This crossroads is where domestic abuse takes a lethal turn for thousands of people. We often think that we know our romantic partners best. But are we really the best judges of character? Remember, people with Stockholm Syndrome don't know they have it! As much as women think they can assess the likelihood that their partner will get violent enough to result in homicide, thousands of cases every year end in exactly this way. The dead can't go back in time. Do we really ever know whether or not someone is capable of murder? What's the likelihood I'm going to wind up dead?

That's the question we must ask. Luckily, there are telltale signs of a psychopath ready to kill. For example, an abuser might dream about suicide or homicide. They often talk endlessly about death. The more the abuser has built up a vision about who, how, when, and where they would murder, the more perilous the situation is for the woman in his life. In addition, if he has recently carried out self-destructive habits (like driving while under the influence of drugs or alcohol) or has been accused of any type of involuntary manslaughter before, it's also highly likely that he is dangerous to be around. Similarly, guns are a red flag. If an abusive man has weapons and has used them or taken steps to use them in the past to ambush or threaten his victims, children, or himself, then the abuser's easy access to deadly force heightens the possibility of an attack. Over 50% of domestic murders are carried out with a firearm. Even more disturbing, a woman is five times more likely to die from a gunshot wound if her partner owns a gun. So, clearly, abusive men with access to weapons is a recipe for disaster.

The likelihood of murder also increases if there are signs that a man is obsessive about his partner or family. An abuser who is over the top about their partner, who either venerates and feels that they can't live without their partner or accepts they are qualified for their partner regardless of any problems in the relationship, is bound to be life-jeopardizing. If a woman speaks out or makes it obvious that she sees no positive future together, then an abuser may decide he'd rather have his partner dead than not at all. Sick, twisted, and gruesome thinking…but the reality for so many women. Prior to this, an abuser will usually strike out in anger. The moment an abuser accepts that his victim really is determined to leave, he will fly into a fiery rage. If he hears that a victim has taken active steps to leave (like calling a battered women's shelter or help hotline), then the probability of an abuser killing is increased.

In Love With A Monster
Life in an Abusive Relationship

Medication and alcohol consumption is the third red flag to watch out for. Consumption of medications or liquor when in a condition of depression or anger can raise the danger of lethality. If an abuser mixes prescription meds or has taken steps to overdose and murder himself, others, the kids, or family members, he must be considered extremely dangerous. Self-destruction often leads to the destruction of others in domestic abuse situations. Sadly, homicide, followed by suicide, is not unheard of.

Lastly, the likelihood of dying at the hands of an abusive partner shoots sky high if he also has a history of animal abuse. Men intent on harming their so-called "loved one" will sometimes do so by attacking her pet. This tactic is twofold; one, there is physical damage to the animal, which instills fear in the woman. And two, the emotional trauma is agonizing. Abusers who take out their rage on pets are more likely to later assault human beings.

To summarize, we can clearly see that, while women suffering from Stockholm Syndrome do not understand their condition, abusive men, on the other hand, most certainly *are* aware of their horrendous crimes! After learning and absorbing this information, I had to ask myself...if the abuser is conscious of his actions, does he just not care enough to change? The answer to this question is what would end up breaking my heart, and yet, ultimately set me on a course to find my emotional freedom from abuse. Because the truth is, abusers — especially narcissists — know exactly what they're doing.

And they do it on purpose. Our attempts to get into the psyche of an abuser fail miserably because we invest an excessive amount of energy attempting to comprehend why somebody might act so wrongly. We concoct logical reasons about why an individual would hurt somebody they love. For example, we argue, "Perhaps he had an awful adolescence?" or "Possibly, his mom didn't cherish him as a little boy" or "People in pain hurt others." We persuade ourselves that "He didn't intend to attack/corrupt/mortify/humiliate/hit/devastate her" as if intent washes away guilt. But it does not!

Be that as it may, we're all adults. The time for childish excuses is long past. Furthermore, abusers will be abusers, narcissists will be narcissists, and criminals will be criminals, regardless of what cover they might be wearing on some random day or what "poor me" story they attempt to sell. Abusers realize what they're doing, and they do it for premeditated reasons. Abusers aren't dumb. They control others through gaslighting, smear campaigns, the use of violence, and psychological torture. To try to comprehend their thinking is pointless. Simply put, we, as a society, must stop pretending that this isn't a serious issue. It is essential to get domestic abuse out in the open where we can talk about it. We need to stop rationalizing why abusers are the way that they are. If we don't, victims of abuse might as well be tossed aside like trash as we abandon them to false notions that the abuse is somehow either deserved, their own fault, or both. It's unacceptable. And it must end.

To turn a blind eye is to fail women everywhere.

Chapter Eighteen

When to Involve the Police

Outing abusers for who (and what) they truly are doesn't require anything other than a mentality shift. Defining abuse requires us to consider things for what they are, and not what we want them to be. We must put together our experiences and treat them as evidence. What happened? How often? Is this relationship more healthy or unhealthy? Am I more often happy or sad? Answering these questions will allow a survivor of abuse to distinguish between what was affection and love, and what has broken down so badly that there is no possibility of mending the relationship because it is no longer a relationship at all...it is a terrifying domestic abuse situation.

This can be a confusing time, indeed. Many women report feeling like there is a haze or fog in front of their eyes that blocks them from making sound and rational decisions. Trust me when I say that any abuser (and particularly, a narcissist) will be okay without you! Unfortunately, there will always be another person to purchase a ticket to that frightful bazaar that an abuser is a ringmaster of. When a woman finally stands up for herself and refuses to be a punching bag, the narcissistic abuser simply goes hunting elsewhere for another victim, like a predator on the prowl. This is all he knows, after all.

In any case, the future of the abuser is no longer a survivor's problem. But getting out can be tricky. As we have learned in prior chapters, many abusive men will stop at nothing to maintain their twisted fantasy that keeps their victims trapped in a predetermined role they have plotted out. Many times, when a woman is on her way out the door, the police end up being called. This could be to report domestic violence, to have a witness stand by and record the ongoings as she attempts to leave, or to ensure her and her children's safety while moving boxes,

In Love With A Monster
Life in an Abusive Relationship

personal objects, clothes, etc. out from the family residence.

Astonishingly, even in the face of the police, abusers will lie and try to twist the facts to suit their narrative. For example, to dominate their partners, abusers sometimes call the police against their victims or injure themselves on purpose, as if they are the ones being harmed! They might deliberately cut themselves, break furniture, or provoke their victim and use threats of physical violence. When a woman hits back or gets physical in an attempt to protect herself, the abuser will cry foul. Now, it is *he* who is injured!

Controlling the story of what happened is the abuser's plan, because it allows him to interact with his victims and law enforcement agencies on his terms, thus, interfering with the victim's ability to get help. He might even go so far as to call the police himself to report that he is being abused, just to turn around the story and keep the spotlight on himself. This is the true nature of an abusive narcissist. People will often ask, "Why didn't she just call 911?"

Well, it's not always that straightforward. And in fact, calling the police can be deadly.

Let's look at an example. The following story is about a woman named Anita. Anita felt like she was losing her mind. Her husband, Sam, had been in

In Love With A Monster
Life in an Abusive Relationship

control of her for many years, screaming, acting violently, and threatening to harm their children. Anita put up with this behavior for years without telling anyone. Anita finally called the police one morning, fearing that Sam might hurt the children. Sam overheard the phone call and locked himself in the bathroom. When police arrived on scene, Sam was bleeding from his chest. He claimed that Anita had attacked him with a knife. He described the wounds on his arms as a result of an earlier fight.

Despite her desperate pleas that this was not an accurate representation of what had happened, the police were not interested in Anita's side of the story (which was the truth) and arrested them both. Anita faced more serious legal charges because Sam had visible wounds. Sam decided to not press charges, and he told Anita that if she ever thought about calling the police again, he would make sure she stayed in jail for life. Anita crumbled into despair. She lost all confidence in the criminal justice system.

As in the example above, self-harm may be used to intimidate victims by threatening them with jail time, child protection inquiries, or worries that their children will disappear in a custody battle. Abusers also hope that this distorted story of abuse will spread further into their mutual acquaintances, family, and society, and thus, tarnish the image and reputation of their victims. The abusers hope that their injury will continue to hamper the relationship.

In Love With A Monster
Life in an Abusive Relationship

It's all part of an intricate plan to manipulate, even at the risk of their own physical well-being. That's how far the abuser will go to maintain control. He'll stop at nothing.

Without a doubt, self-inflicted harm is a form of domestic violence. It is also a form of gaslighting. Fortunately, there are police officers who are trained to spot and understand this complicated topic. One of the workshop participants we read about told listeners that her husband had spoken to police on two separate occasions after attacking her, trying to act like *she* was the criminal. Both times, the police didn't believe her words and argued that there was nothing wrong in their approach to the domestic abuse situation.

Depending on where in the world you are, some legal jurisdictions invalidate "primary aggression preference" laws, which do not require police to know who attacked whom first. This is why it's so important for police to be trained to recognize domestic abuse signals and to know how to respond to a situation where there is clearly an imbalance of power, as well as manipulation tactics, at play.

Chapter Nineteen

The Victim Becomes the Abuser

Among the challenges of understanding abuse is coming to terms with deception. Of course, nobody wants to believe that the person they love is a liar. It's hard to grasp. How could somebody be so shady? So dishonest? Those experiencing domestic

In Love With A Monster
Life in an Abusive Relationship

abuse struggle to understand how the man they live with can, at one second, be so kind, gentle, and sweet, and then bam! Suddenly change into a monster. It's key to remember that individuals who abuse others are frequently victims of abuse themselves – whether that came at the hands of their parents or family members, outsiders, past girlfriends, etc.

This isn't said to excuse the behavior, but rather to show that deception is a learned trait. The incredible tragedy of abuse is that it is cyclical in nature, meaning it gets passed on from one person to another, and another, and another. The weight of breaking the pattern essentially falls on the latest victim.

This feeling of being re-victimized is "typical" in domestic abuse cases. It's also one of the reasons why victims say they accepted the violence for so long – because it was learned and normalized over time.

Elise Franklin, a psychotherapist situated in Los Angeles, says that, "On the off-chance that adoration has been accompanied by abuse for as far back as you can recall, you may not understand that what you're seeing is actually abusive behavior. Somebody who is accustomed to being told, 'You're useless,' may feel oddly comfortable with that information from others, and furthermore, pass on that information as well. We're animals of examples and propensities, and in case we're not careful, we can re-sanction these again and again unwittingly."

Victims of abuse who then later become abusive themselves are totally uninformed that they've mentally switched roles. They don't even recognize that they have turned into the very monster they hate! Years of being undermined, belittled, hated, and mentally, emotionally, and physically hurt have the ability to warp even the most reasonable person's perspective.

Basically, they still consider themselves to be the only victim. We sometimes see this in the case of parent-child abuse relationships. A parent who was abused as a child will then grow up and have children of their own, who they abuse, in turn. But they see no issue with this because, in their minds, they will forever be the main victim, leading them to lash out towards their kids in horrible ways.

Franklin later clarifies this concept by writing, "Being abused is amazingly debilitating, so somebody who has encountered that as a kid would grow up attempting to defeat that sentiment of debilitation, which can, once in a while, transform into them 'overcoming' others." She adds, "Basically, old, stifled annoyance gets transformed into a sort of vengeance, which they take out on others — it's an oblivious message that 'I'm large, and nobody will hurt me once more, and to ensure that I'll hurt others first,' regardless of whether it's their own children or loved ones."

So, the next logical question: why do some victims of abuse go on to do the same to others, even when they have firsthand knowledge of how damaging this is?

German Prevention Network sheds some light on the issue. As quoted by them, "When it comes to breaking the pattern of abuse, moral duty is a pivotal idea." Furthermore, there is a concept called *Kein Täter werden* (signifying, "Don't Offend"). This outlines "assuming liability for one's own conduct" as among the key remedial central focuses for stopping abuse dead in its tracks. As it were, the initial victim must perceive that he or she is currently a grown-up who holds control over others, and assumes liability for the manners by which he/she practices that power." That is to say, a victim of abuse must make a conscious effort to break the cycle. Or else, they will become the very thing they despise the most...

Chapter Twenty

The Deadly Nature of Continued Mental Abuse

Mental abuse and physical abuse both have the potential to be deadly. Yet, society often ignores the more silent killer that is mental abuse. Cuts, bruised arms, and bloody eyes are easy to see. Therefore, labeling somebody as "abusive" because he hits a

In Love With A Monster
Life in an Abusive Relationship

woman isn't hard. But to spot mental abuse takes a careful and dedicated eye, since it's much simpler to hide in plain sight and requires the victim to openly acknowledge her own suffering – which is not always a safe task. In this chapter, we are going to look at the deadly nature of mental abuse.

To start, mental abuse can be defined as actions that can insult someone or lower one's self-esteem. Examples include: making unreasonable demands, criticizing too much, wanting the partner to sacrifice the needs of others, and doubting their ideas and going silent when they do something disagreeable (commonly referred to as gaslighting).

There are many ways in which one can abuse others, but all of the consequences can be equally devastating. Other examples of mental abuse may also include bullying, abusive language, rude nicknames, passive-aggressive backhanded compliments, verbal abuse, and mental manipulation. When a woman realizes that she is being mentally abused, some decide to stay, while others develop unhealthy ways to cope with the trauma.

We mention all of this because mental abuse is often a major component of domestic abuse. Domestic abuse, or co-violence, affects millions of people every day. It has been reported that 84% of people experience psychological abuse at the hands of their romantic partners at some point in their lives– a truly shocking number! Further proof is that as much as society tries to sweep this issue under the rug, it simply cannot be hidden.

Why? Well, we know that the effects of mental abuse can be just as deadly as physical abuse. Mental abuse has a devastating effect on a woman's overall well-being and health. Mental abuse can be direct, with abusers making victims feel inadequate, insecure, and traumatized. Also, mental abuse can trigger emotional helplessness, dependence on the abuser (i.e., financial, as their only support system, etc.). In other cases, people who experience mental abuse can develop disorders, such as anxiety, depression, and post-traumatic stress disorder.

Like all forms of abuse, the victims of mental abuse endure the tirades of their abusers and are often isolated and left to collapse. Abusers will employ a wide variety of techniques to accomplish this. For example, they might ignore the person, constantly lie to them, and cast insults. This all, in turn, develops into a state of extremely negative self-esteem, which affects the victim's mental health.

When does it end? Never, if we allow it. Many abuse cases begin with mental abuse that has devastating effects and eventually leads to emotional and physical abuse. Respect and love for the woman in a domestic abuse situation gets diminished over time until her sense of self and self-worth have been totally obliterated. As a result, the individual in question may believe in self-defeating ideas and become overly self-conscious. Some go on to feel unhealthy in otherwise-healthy relationships with others, like friends and family. Or, they might begin to have a poor relationship with life itself. Suicidal thoughts are not uncommon in domestic abuse cases…sometimes, escape can feel like the only option left (even when it's not!).

And lastly, it is a sad reality that victims of mental abuse sometimes wake up one day hating themselves as they slowly realize that they, too, have learned to display abusive behaviors. Abusers were often abused themselves in the past, and that's why they continue to do so. Sometimes, a woman fleeing abuse is unaware of the harm she can do to others because she is so focused on ensuring her own survival.

But really, can we blame her? No. She was just trying to stay alive.

Chapter Twenty-One

Desperation of the Abuser

Gaslighting falls into the categories of both emotional abuse and mental abuse. People affected by gaslight tactics feel that their lives are in a constant state of chaos. The purpose of gaslighting is to reduce the mental and emotional confidence of the victims. For example, anyone can stand up to their abuser. But what usually ends up happening is the tables get turned.

Suddenly, confronting an abuser about his behavior is met with resistance. An abusive person might say, "You are crazy!" as a way to deflect the negative attention off of himself. In doing so, he forces the victim to question her own line of thinking and ask herself, "Am I really crazy? Am I overreacting? Maybe this isn't so bad." And so, the incident is never reported. As a result, women in domestic abuse relationships may begin to doubt themselves, feel powerless, and lack the confidence to become self-reliant, therefore, never finding the independence to leave the relationship.

Likewise, gaslighting is a form of mental abuse because it can lead to anxiety and depression, low self-esteem and reduced self-assurance, as well as initiate unexpected behavior and stress. Feelings such as these can later lead to difficulties in career advancement, love, and family life, and may require alternate ways to cope. In many of the cases we've seen, this becomes a reliance on drugs and alcohol. Abusers (and especially, mental abusers) use gaslighting to maintain control and break their prey down. In return, the victim internalizes such abuse and develops a toxic relationship with the abuser. It's an intimate and poisonous relationship...one that makes the female victim question her own sanity.

In addition to gaslighting, no book on domestic abuse would be complete without a section on the combination of trauma, mental abuse, and substance abuse. Trauma is often the result of abuse, which can lead to post-traumatic stress disorder (PTSD), complex post-traumatic stress disorder (C-PTSD), depression, borderline personality disorder, suicide, suicidal thoughts, long-term or chronic stress, and eating disorders. Post-Traumatic Stress Disorder includes sleep problems, anxiety, depression, and irritability. Sadly, many women who live to see a life free from abuse still experience the remnants of PTSD long after the relationship has ended. Even isolating themselves from their abuser, or cutting off contact completely, does not instantly get rid of the symptoms of trauma.

According to the statistics on the matter, approximately one-fourth to three-quarters of people who have survived violent traumatic experiences report an alcohol problem. Which is a lot! In the studies, it was reported that women who experienced PTSD were more likely to drink alcohol than those who were not abused.

We are aware that mental abuse causes trauma that can lead to destructive tendencies – alcoholism included. For example, people who have been emotionally, physically, or mentally abused cannot always afford, travel to, or feel comfortable in therapy, and can, instead, develop unhealthy coping

In Love With A Monster
Life in an Abusive Relationship

strategies. These may include drinking, partying, and compulsions such as: gambling, shopping, binge eating, smoking, and the use of harmful drugs. This is called *self-medicating*. However, short-term self-medication strategies can get out of hand and quickly descend into a substance abuse disorder.

Since the lines of what is abusive and what is not are easily blurred to somebody stuck in a toxic relationship, it's essential that we clarify where mental abuse ends and physical begins. It might seem like a silly question, but humor us, and ask yourself: what actually is physical abuse? Where does it start? And where does it end? Is a playful slap on the shoulder that hits a little too hard actually a warning sign? What about a push onto the bed? A rough shove through a doorway? Are these red flags? Or is this already real abuse?

To answer these questions, give the following a quick read.

Physical abuse is basically when a person uses physical force against you. There are hundreds of types of physical abuse, but here, we will highlight only the most common. Physical abuse may be very obvious, like bruising or cutting the victim, pushing or shaking the victim very hard, slapping or kicking the victim hard, choking the victim, throwing objects at the victim…in domestic abuse, such occurrences are normal.

In Love With A Monster
Life in an Abusive Relationship

Even more horrifically, some abusers actually use weapons like knives and guns. Or, they get creative with any object with which to hurt and threaten their victim. It must be mentioned that physically restraining a woman is also a form of physical abuse! Hitting a wall or floor and driving so dangerously in a car that a woman is terrified to be on the road are both quite clearly forms of physical abuse. However, restricting physical movement (such as when a woman is allowed to leave the house or use the bathroom) has the potential to be equally devastating.

To really drive this concept home, let's look to a case study as an example. A 26-year-old woman living in Hermosa, California, was in the news after being beaten with a stick by her boyfriend. When the police were called to the scene, a report was filed detailing the physical abuse that the female victim obviously suffered. They noted her bruised arm, her broken rib, and the cut under her eye.

What they didn't see, however, were the months upon months of seclusion the woman faced as she was denied access to the couple's vehicle. She wasn't permitted to leave the house, go anywhere alone, or make decisions about her own body. But because these aspects of abuse were invisible, it became harder for the police to include anything except anecdotal evidence in their report. In short, they could only lay charges for what they could see with their own two eyes. Again, this proves just how deadly domestic abuse can be, especially when it flies under the radar in circumstances such as this.

Here's another example. There once lived a man and woman who shared an apartment together in Wilmington, Delaware. The woman – let's call her Lola – had a 16-month-old daughter from a previous relationship. Because she was a baby, the daughter would cry and cry and cry endlessly throughout the night. The man (who had a long history of abuse) snapped one evening, angered by the loud noise. He shoved Lola and her infant out the front door and refused to let them back inside the apartment until the baby was quiet. Now, ask yourself: what kind of abuse is this? If you answered both mental and physical, then you would be correct.

No woman ever starts dating a man thinking it will end in abuse. Many survivors of physical abuse say the violence began with a slap or a push but escalated in intensity over time. When in fact, a woman does finally voice her concerns to being treated poorly, one of several things might happen that will make a rational person say, "What? No way!"

First, a victim can be charged. Yup, you read that right. A victim of domestic abuse might end up with a criminal record, all because she objected to enduring abuse. The abuser often accuses someone else, such as the victim, of saying or doing something that caused their violent behavior to start. "She made me do it!" is a phrase we hear over and over again. Or, they may say that their behavior was the result of being under the influence of alcohol or drugs, or of being stressed or frustrated, as if this somehow excuses their actions. But, ask any survivor, and they will say that the abuser was simply lying, just doing this to save himself and protect his own hide. That's not even the most disturbing part. The really twisted thing is...this sometimes works for them.

Next, an abuser will likely let you know that they are "sorry." It is common for the abuser to pretend to feel remorse and apologize after the attack. They apologize and promise that they will never do that again, but after this, they break their promise and, of course, abuse once again. They often express their apologies with much sincerity, which makes it seem as though they actually regret what they have done. To a woman who still has hope that the relationship can be salvaged, it increases the difficulty in leaving the relationship. This is especially true in the early stages of domestic abuse.

Those who successfully escaped look back and wonder how they could have been led so astray. Anybody who has ever been hit before should immediately realize that a little physical assault, however small, is unacceptable. A tiny cut can turn out to be a sign of increasing violence. Pain is undeniable. Abusers may be able to cloud a woman's judgement and convince her that she's "crazy" or "overreacting," but blood dripping down the chin or purple bruises forming up the legs cannot be silenced. As human beings, we will respond to physical pain significantly more proactively than emotional or mental abuse, because it's in our face, impossible to ignore, and something we can instantly *feel*. Unlike the mind or the heart, which can betray us in romantic relationships, physical pain is a definite indicator that something has gone very wrong with the person we are seeing.

However, lots of women find ways to excuse physical abuse too, possibly because they are so used to emotional and mental abuse, that physical harm seems to be the next logical progression of their doomed relationship. Short of a of cataclysmic wound that sends a woman to the ER, emotional torment regularly impacts daily life more clearly than physical pain does. It's not until the pain is so great, so unbearable, that some victims of domestic abuse finally break free of the spell they've been under and say, "This is wrong!"

Now, we have covered a few ongoing themes that make up the most broadly-acknowledged definitions of abuse. Next up, let's join them together here to outline a brief depiction of another technique the abuser will use in his gaslighting experiment - psychological abuse.

In Love With A Monster
Life in an Abusive Relationship

Psychological abuse is any abusive behavior that isn't physical in nature. This may include: verbal animosity, terrorizing, exerting undue control, embarrassment, reducing someone else's feeling of individuality, dignity, and self-esteem, which frequently brings about anxiety, depression, nervousness, melancholy, self-destructive habits or practices, and post-traumatic stress disorder (PTSD). Each of these raise their own challenges. So, in order to better understand the nature of emotional violence, let's dissect what it actually means, piece by piece. In this next chapter, we will examine the psychology of an abuser vs. the psychology of a victim throughout an active domestic abuse relationship.

Chapter Twenty-Two

Inside the Abuser's Head

There are different theories as to why some men abuse those closest to them. One view is that abusers are serious criminals who commit their crimes in a conscious and accountable manner. For these men, they truly believe that they are entitled to act in such despicable ways. The notion of *not* abusing seems strange to them...that's how warped their worldview is. In fact, they might not even see their actions as abusive at all! On the other hand, some abusive men believe that their behavior is a product of deep psychological and developmental scars. For abusers who fall in this latter camp, the argument is that they are not to blame for their actions, since they themselves were once a victim.

Either way, getting inside both of these types of abuser's heads is a fascinating task. Experts have agreed on several commonalities between the two types of domestic abusers. Both groups seek control. Likewise, both are highly manipulative. Each kind of man believes that he, and he alone, is responsible for all aspects of the relationship, from housing to children to marital affairs. Though the first group is more likely to identify with an "alpha male" mentality, at their core, both groups consider themselves victims. The irony of which is – of course – laughable.

For some abusers, violence is a way to prevent a close partner from leaving a relationship or being unfaithful, even if it means physically forcing them to stay. Research shows that, in many cases, acts of domestic violence are behaviors that maintain the status quo. They don't want anything to change. In their heads, the ends justify the means. Abuse is a necessary step they think they must take to maintain their relationship with the other partner, even if she wants out. It doesn't matter. In the mind of the abuser, *he* is in control.

As one abuser explained after therapy, it was all about being overbearing on his victim. He shared, "I could do as I wished. I was trying to scare her. It made it so much easier. I wanted to control her because I knew I could do it. The violence made me feel stronger."

But it wouldn't be fair (or helpful) to spend too much time trying to understand what exactly goes on inside the abuser's brain. For one thing, unless they truly want to change, no amount of education or sympathy will help. And secondly, putting all of our focus and resources on healing the abuser, when in fact, the survivors already do not receive enough attention, funding, and support, would be disingenuous. Therefore, let's shift our focus onto victim psychology for a moment.

Victims of domestic violence need to take time to recognize their situation. Abuse often leaves scars, ranging from injuries and broken bones to difficulty breathing and involuntary tremors. Having more "accidents" than the average person can be a warning sign that someone is being abused. Victims of abuse may also experience short- and long-term emotional and psychological effects, including confusion or a sense of hopelessness, depression, anxiety, panic attacks when out and about in public, and post-traumatic stress disorder (PTSD).

It can take years of therapy to achieve a state of relative peace following a domestic abuse ordeal. Even emotional abuse that isn't physical in nature can break a woman down. Despite how psychological abuse unfurls, specialists in the field all concur that mental abuse affects the individuals who are exposed to it just as badly (if not worse). That's why counseling is a good first step towards a life free of abuse. Physical scars can heal. But mental scars are much more difficult to fix. Tragically, the extent of just how bad the mental and emotional abuse was often isn't known until much later. This makes it hard for a great many people to understand the genuine dangers and harm of psychological abuse, because it can be years or decades in the making. Like a terminal cancer, it silently grows and spreads, infecting the individual without them ever even realizing it.

Again, people wonder, "How? How is it possible that a woman can allow herself to be subjected to such normalized violence and never speak up or act out to fight against it?" It's a fair question. The only real answer is that, if you are lucky enough to have never been the victim of domestic abuse yourself, you probably won't ever understand. At least, not on the same deep level as a survivor.

In Love With A Monster
Life in an Abusive Relationship

For a second, attempt to envision a scene of physical violence. A real battle. Regardless of whether you've never seen or experienced it firsthand, use your mind to be creative. Imagine the fight unfolding before your eyes. The adrenaline and dread. The picture of blood, wounds, tears, screams. It's a difficult thing to imagine, and yet, likely one that you would feel if you were to put yourself in those shoes for just a moment.

Now, let's switch it up. Attempt to picture a scene of psychological abuse. More specifically, somebody whose sense of self-worth has been utterly demolished. Would you be able to see it? No. Of course not. Odds are, your psyche doesn't have the foggiest idea where to start. In any case, on the off-chance that you can make an image of either the demonstrations of abuse or what the harm resembles on the individual who experienced it, would you be able to articulate that picture in words?

We'd be willing to bet that the physical violence was much easier to imagine and describe than the mental abuse. While depicting physical injuries is clear, it's a lot harder to explain emotional harm. The pieces of an individual that were assaulted during the psychological abuse are damaged. This might include personality, dignity, and self-esteem. Each of these three things are conceptual and, thus, very difficult to picture or measure.

In Love With A Monster
Life in an Abusive Relationship

Since psychological abuse is virtually undetectable on the outside, singling out the abuse and pointing fingers at the abuser become challenging tasks indeed.

Even in instances of extraordinary psychological abuse, there are no wounds or slices where the victim can point and state, "This split rib is from that consistent putting down and name-calling" or "That swollen eye and broken lip are from the unending verbal abuse and obsessive lying." Instead, what psychological abuse winds up resembling is an individual who experiences agonizing (yet normalized) suffering and misery.

In conclusion, getting inside the heads of the abuser and the victim provides interesting insights. We have learned that it can be difficult for anybody to see emotional and mental abuse for what it is. The abuser, witnesses, and even the victim herself, often misattribute the harm of abuse. They blame their anxiety and depression on other reasons, like a job loss, family stress, or reoccurring mental health struggles that they dealt with previously. Very rarely does anybody stop to call out an abuser for being the root cause of a victim's mental health decline. Instead, we only focus on the physical. In doing so, we fail to really take in just how deadly psychological abuse can be. As a result, it's carries on in the shadows.

Chapter Twenty-Three

Can You Love an Abuser?

Here's a mind-bending question: can you love an abuser?

The famous fairytale of Beauty and the Beast would argue that, yes, indeed we can. But domestic abuse isn't a Disney movie...it's real life. Some people would debate with this point and say that it stands to reason that, if a woman can come to hate the abusive man in her life, then she can also learn to love him. However, as with all aspects of domestic abuse, the answer is never quite that straightforward. In this chapter, we are going to have a closer look at how survivors of domestic abuse felt before, during, and after abuse took place in their relationships. Ultimately, we want to be able to answer the questions: can you truly love an abuser?

The information that follows comes from various people who have left abusive relationships and who have claimed that they once loved their abusive partner. Since ending the relationships, these women collectively wondered, "What made me love somebody who hurt me so much?" Survivors often cite how bizarre, confounding, and downright wrong it felt to cherish somebody who decided to be abusive. Speaking openly about their experiences helps in two ways. Firstly, to clarify what really happened and examine the emotions for what they are. And secondly, to act as a dire warning: *Get out. Now. Before it's too late.*

Despite these forewarnings, we know that emotions are messy at the best of times. In a domestic abuse situation, feelings like love, sadness, hope, and anger can be even harder to comprehend. Things feel

In Love With A Monster
Life in an Abusive Relationship

weird. You know this isn't what "love" is supposed to look like, and something about the affectionate kisses and cuddles just doesn't seem right. Women usually recognize when that nagging voice inside their head is screaming at them to listen, that something had gone very, very wrong.

Yet, love doesn't just vanish. We can't snap our fingers and make it disappear. It's an association and passionate connection that you make with someone else. Love grows over time. It's built upon trust. Even when abuse starts up, and a woman can clearly see that the love she once shared with her partner is no longer pure, it is difficult to simply pretend like you never loved that person in the first place. They say it takes six months (at minimum) to begin to get over a heartbreak that ends amicably. Now, imagine how challenging freeing oneself from toxic love can be, particularly when the person who is supposed to love you is actually a monster in disguise. Do you have the strength to do it? Hopefully, you will never have to find out.

But in case you, or somebody you know, is battling with sentiments of affection for an abusive partner, early detection is key. Ordinarily, abuse doesn't occur upon immediately seeing someone. Instead, it becomes more prevalent after some time as an abusive partner turns out to be all the more controlling. You may recall the start of the relationship when your partner was enchanting, funny, good-natured, kind and gentle. You may see great characteristics in your partner; he may be an incredible friend to other people, or possibly, a topnotch father, son, or brother.

Until the masks slips off and reveals his true face, the love a woman shares with her abuser *is* real. She's been caught in the trap, but she doesn't know it yet. Therefore, we cannot blame survivors for adoring somebody who they honestly thought was a wonderful person. They were simply tricked.

It starts in small ways. There might be times of "quiet" in the relationship when your partner does something terrible. Say, for example, he gets angry about a phone call you received from a male friend, and in his rage, he throws the cellphone at the wall and accidently shatters it.

At this point, if love is still present in the relationship, the abuser will likely make statements of deep regret, and guarantee that the rash act of violence will never happen again.

Another lie.

During more quiet periods, it may also appear as though your partner has returned to being their "old self" – the brilliant individual they were towards the start of the relationship. You may feel that, on the off-chance that you can always simply do or say the "right" things, the individual you began to look all starry-eyed at would remain, and the abuse would end, permanently.

In truth, there is nothing a woman can say or do to forestall future abuse, in light of the fact that the abuse isn't rooted in her actions. It has nothing to do with the victim, and everything to do with the decisions an abusive man makes. Those times of quiet are regularly used as a strategy that an abusive partner will employ to confuse and control their partner. By acting calm one second and crazy the next, a victim of abuse is kept in a constant state of paranoia and fear. Under these circumstances, nobody would be able to think rationally.

For some victims, feelings of love for an abusive partner can also be a survival strategy. It is hard for a non-abused individual to see how somebody they love, and who professes to cherish them, could hurt or abuse them. To adapt, a victim will often mentally separate from their tormentor subliminally by starting to see things from the abusive partner's point of view.

This survival mechanism gets stronger when an abusive partner utilizes gaslighting strategies to control his victim. The victim slowly starts to agree with the abuser, even against her better judgement! Certain parts of the victim's own beliefs blur after some time. By doing this, the victim figures out how to "pacify" the abusive partner, which may temporarily shield them from being harmed. The need to survive outweighs the loss of their own ability to think independently, especially if a victim relies upon their abusive partner for housing, money, childcare, etc.

Unfortunately, friends, family, and even marriage counselors are sometimes guilty of giving bad advice. A well-intentioned acquaintance might say something like, "Honey, you should try to understand your husband when he expresses his annoyance. It's a sign that he cares about you. That violent behavior will change and show signs of improvement, since you two love each other. Just give it time. Things will improve. You'll see." But how long does one wait? And since when is marital violence ever excusable, especially when it victimizes the woman in the relationship and causes her to be afraid? No. That's not healthy. And no amount of "patience" or "time" will cure a man who is hell-bent on being an abuser.

To be clear, it's normal to feel a sense of love and want to accept your partner, flaws and all. More importantly though, it's critical for women to consider their own security and to realize when, what a partner is giving them isn't really true love at all...but rather a false love. Real love is something that is protected, steady, trusting, and founded upon mutual respect.

In Love With A Monster
Life in an Abusive Relationship

Abuse isn't any of these things; it's all about force and control. It IS conceivable that we sometimes fall in love with somebody and, at the same time, understand that they are definitely not a healthy choice for a long-term commitment. All women have the right to feel safe, valued, and genuinely loved. If a man ever forces you to negotiate on these essentials, the next step is obvious – run.

But what about *after* the abuse has happened? The above scenarios detailed abuse that is ongoing or just beginning. Can love ever be restored after one partner abuses the other?

Remember, abusive relationships (be they physical, psychological, emotional, sexual, etc.) can leave permanent scars. Furthermore, it's not unheard of that these scars can erupt again later down the road. Regardless of how extraordinary and healthy a different romantic relationship may be, it can be hard to put trust in a new partner after experiencing abuse with a previous one. Likewise, it can also be challenging to fully love anybody who has hurt you badly, even though you desperately want to forgive them and forget the incident; the memory of the pain will never entirely fade away…

Ironically, both partners in the relationship might feel that they are powerless to stop psychological and physical abuse. The victim feels trapped, and the abuser feels they cannot (and should not) change their ways. Regardless of who first started the abuse, everybody within its range eventually gets harmed. This includes any children, close family, friends who see what's going on, and of course, the couple themselves. Survivors have shared that their feelings of self-worth and ability to be confident in themselves and happy in future relationships have become damaged. Learning to love again – real love, not abusive, toxic love – requires a long mending process.

So, can somebody learn to love their abuser? No. Abuse is not love. Simple as that. A person can be tricked into believing that what they share with their abusive partner is love, when in fact, it may be denial or a survival mechanism kicking in. We know that abuse and love never go hand-in-hand. Even if during the active relationship, a woman falsely feels that she loves her abuser, there will, no doubt, be a huge number of side effects affecting her health and well-being in negative ways...proof that she needs to re-evaluate.

For example, men who are abusive are skilled at showing passionate verbal and physical articulations of love – for a time. But since the abuse is still present, even intermittently, side effects still slip through the cracks. For example, a woman questioning whether or not it's truly love might also be dealing with: upsetting memories, bad dreams, flashbacks, hyper-cautious nervousness, guilt, blame, surprise reactions, fear of separation, anxiety, and depression. If all of these symptoms are present, chances are high that this isn't love at all. It's abuse.

As a result, many women who have encountered persistent psychological abuse talk about how, later on, they struggle to pick out non-abusive future partners. Their earlier poor relationships make them doubtful that any caring man would ever approach them with genuine kindness. Tragically, they have been conditioned to accept abuse as normal. Accepting that there can't be anything better for them, they may keep on re-picking similar sorts of relationships once more, because they don't know any different. This isn't said to lay blame at the feet of abuse survivors, but rather to highlight the long-lasting effects encountering evil has on a person's psyche.

Similarly, false love affects the body as well as the mind. Recuperating from injuries can't start until the abuse is stopped, either by having the abuser charged or by leaving the relationship. As we know, both of these options are significantly more difficult than one might expect. Numerous victims have been programmed to the point that they are too afraid to even think about challenging their abuser and don't see an approach to getaway. Therefore, if a woman is constantly trying to heal from physical violence but is still unable to leave the source of the violence, her body acts as a sort of "living proof" that this isn't love.

Again, this is not the woman's fault. Experiencing passionate feelings of love happens, normally before we truly know our partner. It's human nature to seek out love and want to be loved in return. Science and biology act as two powers out of our control that urge us to connect with other people and form relationships. So, don't pass judgment on yourself (or others) for loving somebody who doesn't treat his partner with care and regard.

Once a relationship turns abusive, people are still driven by a basic human need to feel loved. There may have been instances of abuse happening early on that got ignored because abusers are experts at enticement and slither along like snakes, until they realize the woman has been snared. Then, and only then, will an abuser reveal his true and horrible nature. By that point, unfortunately, the woman's affection has been solidified. It becomes incredibly hard to leave an abuser.

Don't forget – research shows that it takes, on average, seven attempts to successfully leave an abuser! False love is a big reason why.

Of course, it can feel mortifying to remain in an abusive relationship. There are millions of individuals in the world who don't comprehend this complex issue and cannot fathom as to why a woman would love somebody abusive and why she chooses to stay. There's really no good response. Unless you yourself are intimately familiar with domestic abuse, you will never understand this struggle on the deep level that survivors know all too well.

All we can do is read the writing on the wall – something bad is brewing. Women's rights activist Leslie Morgan Steiner sums it up nicely when she writes, "Domestic abuse happens only in intimate, interdependent, long-term relationships – in other words, the last place we would want or expect to find violence."

Chapter Twenty-Four

Can He Be Forgiven?

The real question is: should a victim stay in an abusive relationship, just because their abuser said, "I'm sorry?"

Sooner or later, everyone must choose. Either stay where you are and concentrate energy on saving the relationship, or prepare to leave. Circumstances

In Love With A Monster
Life in an Abusive Relationship

won't change until a victim decides enough is enough, and as we have learned, that usually comes at the cost of cutting off all association with the abuser. Therapy and counseling can be very helpful when making this tough decision. However, even the best healthcare provider won't be able to settle the issue for you. Of course, they can assist with coming up with an exit strategy and help lay out options, but only the domestic abuse victim will be equipped to comprehend what she truly wants and needs.

Which brings us to (perhaps) the most complicated section of this book. Ultimately, should abusers even be forgiven? Is there ever a situation in which long-term, sustained, violent abuse can be overlooked, swept under the rug, and forgotten? Prior chapters told us no; this is never okay. Yet, to simply shrug our shoulders and pretend that it doesn't happen all the time would be naïve. Women stay in abusive relationships all their lives, and some do report that the abuse stopped eventually. In no way are we condoning this "wait and see" mentality. Rather, our objective is to do as we have always done – face the complex and deeply disturbing issue head-on! So, what do you think? Should abusers ever be forgiven?

Start by asking yourself the following questions. Have you been so badly hurt by someone important to you, to the point of where there really is no conceivable way you will ever be able to forgive that person? Has the crime against you been so heinous that it seems foolish to even consider forgiveness? Do you feel conflicted, wondering if you have to forgive in order to heal yourself (or him)? Or do you wonder if forgiveness is just a way of letting your partner "get away with it?"

If these all seem impossible to answer, good. That's the point! For women trapped in cycles of domestic abuse, thoughts such as these can be a daily occurrence. Unlike in a healthy relationship, the woman usually isn't able to openly discuss her fears and concerns with her partner, which makes trying to draw conclusions an excruciatingly lonely task. Perhaps, this is why it takes so very long for most victims to end things. They are really, truly, totally...alone.

Forgiveness is not easy, no matter how badly you have been hurt. But the ability to forgive – once achieved – is definitely healing. Regardless of how it impacts the abuser, the focus of forgiveness should always include the well-being of both parties involved. Just because a victim forgives her abuser for a transgression, doesn't mean it never happened (hold on – we will go much deeper into this topic shortly). Before I go on, let me reiterate a few quick facts about forgiveness.

To start, forgiveness is not the same as reconciliation. It also isn't something you *have* to feel like doing in order to do, meaning you can still be angry, sad, hurt, AND capable of forgiveness. The two feelings aren't mutually exclusive. Forgiveness is not a step you take in order to avoid feeling the impact of the damage. Rather than being hollow lip service, genuine forgiveness comes from the heart. Nobody can force forgiveness upon you – though narcissists and abusers will certainly try! Many people wrongly assume that forgiveness is the same as forgetting. It's not! Actually, you may never forget what happened to you. Even if you desperately wish you could. Just because you forgive someone, that does not mean you gain instant amnesia. The memory of the hurt will always be there, like a nagging bruise.

Sometimes, abusive people will argue that forgiveness is somehow related to fairness. For example, the line, "I forgave you for calling me a crazy liar! Therefore, you MUST forgive me for slamming the door on your hand, screaming at the baby, pushing you down the stairwell..." (take your pick). In reality, true forgiveness has nothing to do with fairness.

One of the problems people have with forgiveness is that they feel that it isn't fair to ignore the fact that someone hurt them. People who have been hurt feel a need to advocate for themselves by being angry at the perpetrator for the injustice he/she has committed against them. It feels empowering to hold on to anger. It is scary to lay down one's anger and "let go." We feel as though we are sacrificing our hard-won power, which we are entitled to! This is a totally normal feeling, but a toxic one. Particularly in domestic abuse situations.

At this point in the book, we are experts in profiling the abuser. Now, we are going to move on and learn about healing concepts in regards to domestic abuse. Why is forgiveness necessary for healing? Some people cringe at the idea. They see no benefits in forgiving someone who has wronged them deeply. However, science tells us that there are many benefits to be gained from forgiveness, but the primary one is freedom.

Yup, you read that right. Forgiveness isn't just healing…it's a ticket to freedom. Once you have "worked through" the steps of healing from abuse, the final frontier involves laying down your right for justice, fairness, and restitution. In a nutshell, forgiveness is giving you the gift of freedom; the freedom of letting go. Forgiveness is the freedom of saying, "I'm moving on" from the arguing, the violence, and the mental, physical, and emotional assault on one's entire personhood.

One major benefit for a victim's life post-forgiveness is that it stops the "superhighway" in your mind of negativity. When a woman chooses to forgive, she no longer needs to rehearse the crimes committed against her over and over in her head. The abuser

In Love With A Monster
Life in an Abusive Relationship

does not occupy her primary thoughts anymore! She stops needing to assume the worst about her abuser because, quite simply, his nonsense is no longer her problem. To the escaped woman who has given herself the ability to live free from the captivity of needing to hold another person accountable forever, forgiveness is like gold. Hard to find. But so valuable.

However, healing and forgiveness come at a cost. Even if a woman flees the abuse and manages to get to a point where her mind is no longer obsessed with thinking about the toxic relationship, she sometimes needs months or years to reach a place of pure peace. She will occasionally wonder, "Can he still change?" and "Maybe if I go back, and say that I forgive him, things will be different next time." To which the abuser excitedly replies, "Yes! I promise I'll change! Just come back, be mine again, fall into this trap I have set for you..."

The promise of a change in behavior are the words many people in a relationship with an abusive partner have most likely heard. Ached for and, yet, feared, the words offer a victim both expectation and dissatisfaction. Expectation that things truly will improve this time around, and frustration when, unavoidably, the terrible abuse — whether emotional, physical, or verbal—starts once more. We have all heard the old saying that a panther can't change its spots. And hopefully by now, you know that's the case 99% of the time.

Chapter Twenty-Five

Change Isn't Easy

Okay, that's the lived experiences of women who have survived domestic abuse. What does the research actually say on the matter? Shouldn't something be said on the part of the abuser himself? Numerous specialists state that it is possible for abusers to change. However, the change must be wanted. Oftentimes, there are bogus vows to change, concocted as lies and intended to trick victims into staying put in very damaging situations.

So, how would a woman know when a promise to change is genuine—or when it's only an empty guarantee? In all actuality, there's no one driving force that will make an abusive individual change his ways. What's more, as much as you may think about your accomplice and wish things were different, nobody can "make" any other person change by any stretch of the imagination. At the end of the day, they need to take on the internal emotional work themselves. Be that as it may, there are a few signs we can keep an eye out for to differentiate a false promise from an authentic yearning to do better.

Genuine responsibility starts when the abuser recognizes their ways of acting is wrong, truly focuses on changing, and prioritizes the emotions, needs, and wants of their victims over their own selfish ways. While change is feasible, it's difficult to do, and it requires some serious investment. Women who have barely gotten out with their lives intact know this: everybody deserves to live in state of well-being, be respected, and feel loved. Nobody can make any other person change against their will. Be that as it may, it's never too late for a woman who has been abuse to start thinking about herself. She can choose to lead a cheerful, peaceful, and free life. This includes deciding whether, when, and how to leave a bad relationship. What's more, even if a man refuses to change, a woman can still adore herself with all the tolerance, enthusiasm, and fierceness. Just because an abuser is stuck, doesn't mean his victim has to be too.

If a person is violent towards you all the time, it should be easy to see that something in the relationship simply isn't right. And yet, many women are blind. What a great many people who haven't been in an abusive relationship neglect to comprehend is that abusers aren't really barbarians, and they don't act out in obviously savage ways all the time. They can have moments where they act beguiling, sweet, and kind — a key reason behind why abuse victims stay.

The promise of progress can sneak into the woman's thoughts like a snake, whispering guarantees of trust and that, perhaps, this time, things will finally show signs of improvement. Expectation is planted like a seed. It can be a wonderful thing when somebody makes a commitment to bettering themselves, and just because a relationship isn't perfect, doesn't mean that it's doomed to fail, necessarily. Change and forgiveness are both a demonstration of your good faith and flexibility.

However, without a genuine urge to change, the pattern of abuse will probably proceed, no matter how forgiving the victim may be. That is the reason it's imperative to concentrate, not on what abusive people say, but rather, what they do. Actions speak louder than words, after all! Change is possible, but it's hard. Once a woman gets to the point where her abuser is putting himself first and offering up vague promises to change, but not showing any real progress, then we know there's a major problem. Saying, "I forgive you" or "I believe that you have the power to change!" isn't helping anyone. What's more, a woman's affection, idealism, and flexibility might actually be better spent on herself! By giving herself all the adoration, care, and guarantee of a peaceful future she deserves, the abuser is removed from the equation. Change your ways...or don't. Either way, she's (hopefully) moving on!

In addition, when talking about change, we must look at the conditions that make up the environment where abuse takes place. Remember, abuse doesn't happen in isolation. There are always telltale signs. And likewise, there are easy to spot indicators that will let us know whether or not an abuser is serious about changing his behavior. So, when would change truly be able to occur?

To answer this question, let's go back in time for a moment. We already know that abusers typically were abused, oppressed, or injured in some way in their past. Furthermore, particularly for men, there are stereotypes and gender norms which encourage males to act a certain way toward females in society. Unlearning these practices is troublesome. It can take months (or even years) to begin to unlearn these harmful habits. And it's only possibly when the abusive individual completely focuses on surrendering his past attitudes and commits to learning new ones.

Similarly, change is only possible when there is a shift in perspective. In order for an abuser to get better, he must quit focusing on himself. Narcissists are notoriously self-centered. But abusers who have undergone therapy and recovered often report that it was when they first started to feel genuine sympathy for their victims, that real change happened. In this case, they will perceive the deep damage they caused to another absolutely innocent person.

Furthermore, they will assume liability for the abuse, and will take an interest in any procedure the victim wishes to sanction to hold them responsible. This might include having charges pressed, going to court, agreeing to separate, or engaging in couple's counseling. Even if a victim says, "I want to be alone," an abuser who is committed to change will accept this. If a woman asks for no contact, and her partner respects her wishes, he will – and should – leave her be.

And lastly, an abuser who really wants to change doesn't go looking for rewards! He won't expect any sort of remuneration or honor for "good conduct." After all, not being a monster shouldn't win you an award — it's the bare minimum of being a decent human being. In any case, simply acknowledging the need to change isn't sufficient on its own. The process of truly changing hurtful practices is a long, slow, and troublesome road to go down. It can take a lifetime to learn how to be abusive, so unlearning those practices — while absolutely doable — takes a hell of a great deal of work! This work doesn't have to done in isolation, however. It can occur via programs explicitly intended to help abusers see their bad ways clearly and learn new, healthier examples of how to live. Abusers who truly want to change will likewise address concurrent issues — like drug or alcohol abuse — by looking for qualified, long-term support.

At the end of the day, change isn't easy. For men and women stuck in a domestic abuse situation, the information really boils down to this: do I stay and wait for him to change? Or do I change the situation myself, by ending things? The choice is yours.

Chapter Twenty-Six

The Psychological Warfare of Abuse

For an outsider looking in, domestic abuse seems crazy. How on earth could any self-respecting person allow another to treat her so poorly? We wonder and look on with a sort of appalled curiously. On the outside, domestic abuse is a clear sign to leave the relationship, but for those going through it, it's much harder to just walk away, especially if there's a long history between the two partners. In this chapter, we are going to jump in and examine the nitty gritty of the psychology behind why women stay, even after the abuser has proven that he *clearly* has no intention of ever changing.

The mental reasons why women remain are normally less obvious, making it difficult for some to comprehend and feel empathy for victims. But we must try! Thousands of women die at the hands of their abusers each and every year. To shrug our shoulders and go, "Well, if she had it so bad, why didn't she just leave?" accomplished absolutely nothing. Actually, it's a form of victim blaming which perpetuates the cycle and enables the sick mentalities of abuse to continue.

Usually, the first thought that crosses a woman's mind when it comes to abuse is that the violence is somehow her fault. They erroneously believe that something must not be right with themselves. The most common reaction? To assume responsibility for the violence and carry it as their own shameful burden, depicting the first stage a woman normally experiences when she thinks something must be wrong within her. Her reaction? "Thus, I took a shot at myself and remained." She, at that point, portrayed different reasons for taking the blame. She says, "In the event that he was a beast constantly, maybe it would have been simpler to leave. Be that as it may, he could be benevolent and touchy. Thus, I remained."

Similar reports are made by domestic abuse survivors. We have heard those that got free say things like, "He cried and said he was sorry. So, I figured it was my overreaction." Or, "He offered to find support and even went to a couple of meetings and treatment gatherings. I never went to therapy. Maybe I am the problem in this relationship." Similarly, the notion that, "He tore down my knowledge and crushed my self-esteem and sense of certainty. That's why I remained. I felt embarrassed and caught." In all of these examples, the victim blames herself. Again, this states facts that we have also found in our research: that abusers change from showing extraordinary kindness and consideration to being a beast; that the victim feels empathy when the abuser apologizes, even though the apology is false; and that the victim clutches to the naïve trust that the abuser will change.

Remember, women will make approximately seven attempts to leave an abuser before cutting off the relationship completely. There are such a significant number of conceivable, singular conditions compelling a victim's capacity to either end things…or not. Self-blame is a top reason why so many find it impossible break free. That's because domestic abuse is complicated! As we discovered in prior chapters, it is possible to both love a person and still hate what they do to you. In this next section, let's further investigate the dark and conflicting emotions felt by victims of domestic abuse.

There are different ways in which emotions can strain against one another. Fear and love. Trust and shame. Resentment and hope. The internal conflict a victim feels can be intense. Many survivors report that living in their domestic abuse situation was akin to psychological warfare! Consider a couple of emotions at odds with one another. For example, dread and interest. They might compete against one another if they happen to join on something very similar. The more I am interested in a snake charmer's controls of a venomous reptile, the more frightful I am of him being bitten, right? The same idea applies to domestic abuse cases.

Next, consider happiness and misery. Doubtlessly, the brain could be conflicted between these two sets of emotions. On one hand, a victim might feel extraordinarily happy with her partner when things are good, the bills are paid, the kids are content, and there is no stress in the relationship. However, as we have learned, the pendulum can quickly swing in the opposite direction. Suddenly, everybody is miserable! When it comes to healthy relationships, these conflicting emotions might occur, but not drastically. They don't go from bliss to horror within hours (or even minutes). But, in a domestic abuse situation, emotions are all over the place. This is done intentionally, to keep the victim in a constant state of confusion and unrest. If she's too busy trying to figure out why she feels the way she does – and what she might have done to cause a fight or argument – she won't have time to evaluate the relationship clearly. Therefore, keeping the abuser 100% in control.

To summarize, contradictory emotions are normal. Various emotions may mix, become so entwined that they produce an alternate feeling (for example, love for somebody and frightfulness of losing her warmth may produce envy). In different types of ongoing domestic conflict, one might truly feel two emotions at the same time, and neither appears to rule the other! We can use a metaphor to illustrate this concept. For example, consider an outdoorsy adventurer who scales a precarious mountain in the Alps. This person will need to navigate dangerous bluffs. As a result, she may feel dread from the threat of falling. Mountains can be scary, even for experienced climbers! However, the person might simultaneously feel awe and self-admiration from getting over the precipice to see the lovely view.

Add to the dread and enchantment, she might also be overwhelmed by a feeling of puzzlement. This swirling of emotions is a universal experience. As human beings, we are complicated! Positive and negative feelings can coincide. The main reason why we bring up this example here is to show that multiple viewpoints about the same situation are possible. Sure, negative circumstances will prompt negative emotions, and a positive experience will prompts positive ones.

But these feelings need not be concurrent and may lead to a mix of even more complicated emotions! Think about skydiving. We can envision that a skydiver encounters fear, but additionally, passion or pride from achieving a thrilling undertaking. The experience of the two emotions could be seen as the coupling, of sorts. The co-event of dread and fervor makes one search out skydiving because, even though a negative feeling is encountered, the simultaneous positive feeling is more grounded than the negative feeling.

Why do we bring up these imaginary scenarios? Well, because our brains work the same way! We can feel two opposing emotions at the same time. By extension then, the same logic can be applied to victims (and perpetrators) of domestic abuse. The following are some reasons why victims have conflicting emotions. To start, fear. A woman may be afraid of what will happen if she decides to leave the relationship. If she has been threatened by her partner, family, or friends, she especially may not feel safe leaving. As well, in this made-up situation, let's pretend the house is in her husband's name. So, she's terrified, but also feels angry at the thought of potentially being forced out of her own home. Again, two emotions. Equally valid.

Fear is rarely the only emotion a victim feels. Almost always, it's accompanied by deeper emotions. After all, what does the fear stem from? There must be a reason. If a woman doesn't know what a healthy relationship looks like, perhaps from growing up in an environment where abuse was common, then she may not recognize that her relationship is unhealthy. Therefore, when well-meaning friends point out that they don't approve of the rude manner in which her boyfriend publicly shames the ways she dresses and speaks, she might feel embarrassed, but also defensive of her relationship. It's absolutely possible for the brain to get so warped by abuse, that the victim ends up defending the actions of her abuser!

This is more common than you might think…All because of scattered emotions. In this case, it's probably hard for the women to admit that they've been abused. They may feel that they've done something wrong by becoming involved with an abusive partner in the first place. They may also worry that their friends and family will judge them. Thus, worry, defensiveness, anger, embarrassment, and fear all build and form the perfect storm, blocking a victim from seeing clearly as they try to navigate these complex emotions.

We should also note, of course, that domestic abuse occurs in LGBTQ+ relationships too. The fear of being outed prematurely (or at work) can be a very strong emotional motivator.

If a person is LGBTQ+ and has not yet come out to everyone in their circles, their partner may threaten to reveal this secret. Being outed may feel especially scary for young people who are just beginning to explore their sexuality. There may be some remnants of embarrassment.

It's probably hard for a LGBTQ+ victim of abuse to admit that they've been abused, since this is a topic many people don't talk openly about. They may feel like they've done something wrong by picking a less than stellar partner. They may also worry that their friends and family will judge them whether they stay or leave. Humiliation and fear are often cited as main reasons why people don't leave.

Last, is low-esteem. If a woman's partner constantly puts her down and blames her, it can be all too easy to believe those statements and think that the abuse is her fault. Weeks, month, and years of such belittling can erode confidence. The resulting emotions are depression, anxiety, and often shyness. Yet, a victim may still say she loves her abuser! Of all the emotions, love is the strongest. She may stay in an abusive relationship hoping that her abuser will change…all because she "loves" him. Think about it

In Love With A Monster
Life in an Abusive Relationship

— if a person you love tells you they'll change, you desperately want to believe them, don't you? Victims of domestic abuse may only want the violence to stop, not the relationship to end entirely. This complicated fact is the heart of the issue.

To summarize, domestic abuse is much more complicated than we think. For most women, becoming a victim is something they never dreamt of! Who would have thought they'd become a statistic? You never think it will happen to you, until it does. It very well may be a complicated, confounding, baffling, threatening, and terrifying experience. The pressure of waking up and realizing that this is your life now can be a shattering feeling.

That's why getting out early is critical.

Chapter Twenty-Seven

It's Over. Now What?

Finally. The day has come. The woman being abused has decided to switch her mentality. No longer will she call herself a "victim." From now on, she is a "survivor."

In Love With A Monster
Life in an Abusive Relationship

Unfortunately, it's not quite so easy as that. Ending an abusive relationship carries many risks. Pressure can come from all angles. Often, there are threats and intimidation once a woman makes it clear that she is leaving. Naturally, this overwhelming strain only adds to the framework of a victim's injury. And what's more, sometimes it's necessary to involve the law. Especially when mutual assets (like cars and houses) are involved, or when there are custody issues over children, then lawyers might need to be enlisted. While the criminal justice system doesn't have structures in place to support women who are fleeing abusive partners, ultimately, much of the work rests squarely on the victim's shoulder. This is an exhausting – and dangerous – time.

Since a woman's risk by and large increases as she attempts to get away from her abuser, it is imperative that she has a well-considered security plan. She is the master of her circumstance and has been utilizing every last bit of her aptitudes to survive up until now. The probability is high that her abuser will fight back or that the brutality will increase as she attempts to build a better life for herself. Remember, talking openly about the violent behavior of an abuser can be a terrifying and perilous thing for a survivor to do. If she has left the shared living accommodation already, the courtroom may be the first occasion when she faces her accomplice since the last assault took place, or since whenever she had the opportunity to leave. Rage, disgust, fear, and sadness all bubble just below the surface.

We know that getting free is always worth the struggle. A life of violent abuse is no life at all. Yet, society regularly overlooks the steps a victim must take in order to say, "That's it. I'm truly done this time. It's over." Women who have successfully ended things report that the annoyance (and viciousness) of their abuser was heightened because of the means she took to free herself. Since victims perceive the peril related to standing up against their abusers, and know full well the very real dangers of doing so, they may purposely deny allegations of abuse or decline to help investigators and police who have been assigned to the case.

This is especially true after an assault. While declining to collaborate may give off an impression of being irrational, it's actually part of many victims' escape plans. Should an abuser be sent to prison, he can't hurt her—for a while. But abusers regularly hold long grudges and have methods of controlling their victims even while imprisoned (e.g., utilizing companions, family, or children to do their dirty work/exercise fear and control). If this sounds horrifying…that's the point. This is exactly what happens every single day all around the world.

Furthermore, the individuals who do go to prison may still look for retribution once they are discharged. Even if a restraining order is filed, some abusers will nonetheless try to get in contact with their past victims. Recall, the rules don't apply to them! In their minds, they are the hero of the story. A piece of paper that says, "Stay away from ____" means diddly squat to them. To give some perspective, consider the follow statistic. Following the end of an abusive relationship, psychological abuse is still typical, with 11.2 percent of women at WSU revealing being engaged in a sincerely damaging personal relationship, as indicated by the American College Health Association.

The other thing to keep in mind is that leaving takes time. The relationship might be over, yes. But that doesn't mean that a woman can just pack up her life and find a new job, new housing, and new support systems overnight. These things take time! So, while she is planning her exit, abusers will try to turn the tables, so to speak. They will frequently confine the victim, preventing them from reaching out to companions or helpful individuals.

Phones might be disconnected. The car keys go missing. They refuse to look after the kids. Nasty tactics such as these are ways the abuser tries to seize control, once he realizes the game is ending. In the same way, abusers may likewise be profoundly possessive or manipulative, causing all sorts of relationship issues for the victim. They might try to provoke an outburst, taunting appearances like hair, clothes, weight, exercise habits, or any part of the victim's body, and tell the victim that she merits the abuse or makes the abuser act the way he does. Again, this is a hasty grab at control. He knows it's over. That's why he's suddenly fighting so hard.

In any case, this is just further abuse in and of itself. Plain and simple. It doesn't take physical brutality for a relationship to be abusive. Refusing to let somebody leave – or actively engaging in behavior that makes their exit more difficult – proves just how rotten the mentality of domestic abusers really is. A considerable lot of these variables play into why a victim doesn't leave a relationship quickly. The issue is significantly more complicated than our victim-blaming society generally accepts. "Why didn't she just bolt?" we ask. When really, what we should be saying is, "Oh my gosh! Look at how many obstacles he put in her way before she could get free!" It's a sad reality that we live amongst a public who likes to lay blame at the feet of the survivors. If we are honest with ourselves, the real obligation ought to be with the individual who decided to abuse his partner in the first place.

Ultimately, we have to understand that abusive behavior in the home is substantially more complicated than we might suspect it to be. There are a bunch of reasons individuals remain in a toxic domestic abuse relationship, many of which we have covered in earlier chapters. Particularly on a mutual acquaintance and family grounds, victims and abusers frequently have similar social circles. This can lead to disagreements. People pick sides. Not everyone will agree with the victim. If mutual friends or family members side with the abuser, then they may try to convince the person being abused to stay, either loudly or in more insidious ways. Victims might be so undermined by this that they don't think there is anything else they can do.

When society, your friends, your family, and your entire social unit is telling you to do one thing, even though you know it's unhealthy, it can be an excruciatingly painful experience. Also, to be blunt, many individuals simply don't have the foggiest idea of what a truly healthy relationship resembles. Ever heard of the saying, "Misery loves company?" Basically, this means that some people are unhappy in their marriages and dating lives, and so, they enjoy dragging down others with them. We like to think that all of our friends and family will be supportive of our choice to leave, but sadly, this isn't always the way it pans out.

Really, the choice to leave is a lonely path. Hopefully, a victim will be lucky enough to have one or two very supportive people in her life to ease the transition. However, it's clear that people tend to obscure and bury the truth. In general, we don't talk about domestic violence. Especially not within our own families! It's viewed as impolite and even unacceptable to discuss these things in school, at work, or over dinner...because acknowledging the horrors of domestic abuse would be admitting we are in crisis mode. So, we choose comfort. We stay silent. We let innocent women die at the hands of their abusers.

How incredibly tragic.

Chapter Twenty-Eight

Premeditated Abuse: Steps Abusers Take to Hurt Others

Let's get something straight – abuse is methodical. A person who chooses to abuse others emotionally, physically, or mentally knows exactly what they are doing. Unlike children, who are still learning and growing, when a grown man hits somebody, he can't feign ignorance. He knows that what he did was wrong, is aware of the effect it will have on the person he is assaulting, and understands the potential consequences of acting this way. Just like a spider, he weaves his web. Then, he waits to stalk his ideal prey, who is totally clueless to the dangers she's in...

It really does happen kind of like that. When a couple gets married, people will often refer to the time period immediately after the ceremony as the "honeymoon." This is when a couple is head over heels in love! The romance is fresh. Each partner is wearing rose-colored glasses. Everything feels special, magical, and perfect. It should be a wonderful and intimate time. And yet, for so many women, this is where their new life of domestic bliss makes a dark U-turn. In this chapter, we are going to figure out why the so-called "honeymoon" stage ends, and what steps an abuser takes to plan out his future reign of terror. Ready? Let's start.

First, the honeymoon stage ends. This might be abrupt or more drawn out, depending on the abuser's tactics of choice. A partner who abuses relies upon aggression, coercion, or violence to exert control. Abuse is a power game designed to show you who the boss is. Typically, it starts small. A rude comment here. An eye roll there. Maybe a light

In Love With A Monster
Life in an Abusive Relationship

whack on the arm that later gets harder, more forceful, begins to leave a purple bruise. The millisecond a woman tells her partner that she isn't pleased with this behavior (and he argues back) is also the same moment the honeymoon stage ends.

Next up is guilt. Now that the abuser has exerted some control in the relationship, he knows that he must invoke feelings of guilt in order to daze and confuse his victim. At this point, she is still madly in love. But there is a tiny nagging voice at the back of her head yelling a red flag warning that something is wrong. After hurting her, the abuser will likely pretend to feel guilty about himself (alas, he does not!) In reality, he simply worries about being caught and facing the consequences of his misconduct. "Sorry," the abuser cries. "I feel so awful!" In this way, the abuser justifies whatever he did. An abusive individual might also come up with excuses. Either way, he will refuse to accept responsibility. If the domestic abuse situation is really heating up and beginning to spiral out of control, he might even accuse his victim of being in the wrong!

Then, the abuse gets normalized. The abuser makes every effort to regain control and keep the victim in the relationship. He can act as if nothing has happened, or he can turn his attention away. This short return to a peaceful "honeymoon-like" stage can give the victim hope that the abuser has changed this time. Sadly, it doesn't last. Your abuser will start thinking about abusing you once again. He's addicted – like a drug. He spends a lot of time thinking about what *you* did wrong and how he will now pay you back. He then intends to turn the concept of abuse into reality...a living Hell, of sorts.

At this point in the domestic abuse scenario, the stage has been set. The roles are clearly defined. The abuser gets to rant, rage, and throw temper tantrums while the victim shrinks into the shadows. Everything has gone according to the abuser's plan. He has created a situation where he can justify abusing you. As a result, it can be difficult to accept apologetic gestures. An abuser will assure you that you are the only person who can help him, that this time, things will be different and that he loves you. However, the risks to life are very high. Sometimes, there's a threat of physical violence if the victim does not comply. Once this starts happening on the regular, it almost never ends. After an attack, abusers usually cry crocodile tears and will say how sorry they are and promise that they will never repeat what they did.

Don't believe their false promises.

Oftentimes, it can be hard for people who are unfamiliar with domestic abuse to relate to those who have lived experiences of it. Suffering is a universal experience, yes. However, domestic abuse is a particular kind of evil. There is power to be

In Love With A Monster
Life in an Abusive Relationship

found in sharing stories of survival. In the spirit of this, and to illustrate just how carefully an abuser sets his traps, we now turn to the story of Eileen.

Eileen was a beautiful young woman. She had just graduated from college. Her grades were excellent, and so, it was no surprise to everyone when she was offered a high-paying job at one of the leading businesses in her downtown city. During her first week at the new job, she met a man named Scott. He worked on the same floor. Right away, the two hit it off! Scott was funny, smart, and had a good sense of humor. He loved to make Eileen laugh. She recalls, "It was amazing at the beginning. We were so great together. But then it started to slowly change. At first, I thought it was because of the romance and attention, which I wasn't accustomed to, that things felt a bit off."

Shortly after, Scott began to pester Eileen. He would always ask where she was going and who she was with. "I just want to know that you're safe," Scott would say. Which, in Eileen's mind, made sense! He was just being a caring guy, right? She shrugged it off and acted as if everything was fine. Then, Eileen said, "But early one morning after a night out, I woke up at a friend's house, and he began yelling at me. He accused me of being in bed with someone else. I wasn't – I had just been unable to get a taxi. After I tried to explain that my friend was at home, not another man, he just kept shouting. He told me that I did not have the right to treat him that way. I thought he was confused, and he must have thought I was really with someone else. So, I tried to calm him down. Somehow, his behavior was explained away, and I thought it was a blip. After hours of shouting, he finally let it go. I was surprised and hurt, but figured his reaction was mostly one of jealousy...not a red flag for abuse."

Eileen continues, "After a few weeks had passed, we got home from a party we were at together. He started yelling at me again, told me I made a show of it with the men at the party. That night, he hit me for the very first time, and then it became part of the routine. Over time, I learned that being alone with my friends or socializing with him just wasn't worth a beating afterwards. Even when he went out, he would call me to check up on me. Where I was, and who I was with, always needed to be documented. I had to make sure I picked up the phone when he demanded it."

"Over time the controlling behavior worsened. It became about more than just going out. He took our shared money and said I was talking nonsense about the finances when I expressed concern about how he was spending it. So bad that, in the end, I gave up my job. The anxiety of being worried about his reaction all the time crushed me. I was so lonely. And so embarrassed. But I didn't know how to escape. And when I got pregnant, it just seemed like my life was over. That it was always going to happen this way. I totally collapsed. I didn't know who I was anymore."

Now, seeing the domestic abuse for what it was, Eileen had a choice to make. Like all abusers, Scott had carefully laid out the steps he would take to entrap her. Which he successfully did! But Eileen's eyes had been opened. She decided she had to leave, for her own health, and for the sake of her unborn baby.

She reflects, "When I finally left during another attack, he threw a bottle at me, and it terrified me that he would do such a horrific thing. The next day, I told my mother and sister that I needed help. It was the hardest thing to do. My sister helped me find the right support, and now, I'm away from the abuse. I filed a court order against Scott. It was hard work. The court is not easy at all to navigate. Actually, it was probably harder than just living with the abuse and putting up with it, but in my case, it's worth it. My life is no longer in danger now, my baby is happy, and I look forward to every day instead of waking up in fear. If I can advise anyone else, it's just to tell someone: Don't try and deal with it yourself, and don't try and keep it a secret…because you don't need to."

In this real-life scenario, we can see how a perfectly independent and strong woman was taken advantage of. Abusers are trained and know exactly what (and who) to look for in their victims. They don't choose at random. The abuse is premeditated. Scott took the steps necessary to lock in Eileen. He love bombed her, made the relationship official quickly, isolated her from friends, took control of the finances, and restricted her movement, all before using a pregnancy as a last-ditch resort to try and keep her from leaving.

What he didn't count on, of course, was that Eileen would fight back.

Chapter Twenty-Nine

Time to Put Our Knowledge to the Test

There are two sides to every story. And though the truth isn't subjective, it often feels that way. Nowhere is this more evident than in domestic abuse cases! When family, friends, and prosecutors look at domestic abuse, they are often left staring from the outside in. Only the two people directly involved in the abusive situation know exactly what is going on, and even then, the mental states of each party are sometimes so distraught, so riddled by confusion, anger, and fear, that even they themselves find navigating the way forward to be a difficult undertaking. In this final chapter, we are going to try something completely different. Up until now, information has been put forth in an educational sort of way to highlight the horrors of domestic abuse.

Now, we ask you – the reader – to actively participate! Here, we are going to examine the two sides of a domestic abuse case; his and hers. It will be *your* job as a neutral third-party witness to imagine yourself in the shoes of each individual, both as the abuser and the victim. We will then prompt you to draw conclusions and identify which types of abuse are taking place, why, and what the likely outcome of the scenario will ultimately be given the information provided.

Again, let us offer a sensitivity warning. This next section may be emotionally triggering for some readers, especially those who have experiences with violence. If you find yourself needing support, please stop reading immediately, and go seek help from your support system.

Ready to get reading? Buckle up. Here we go.

In Love With A Monster
Life in an Abusive Relationship

POV: The Abuser

First, we start from the perspective of the abuser (not because his story is more important than the victim's story, but simply to lay the groundwork for what is to come). For the sake of this scenario, let's call our abuser "Paul." A little bit of history: Paul is a twenty-nine-year-old young man. He is employed by a hospital. This is one of the busiest wards in the city, and Paul works nightshifts as an emergency room nurse. His job is stressful, to put it lightly.

All evening and into the wee hours of the morning, Paul helps to treat people suffering from car accidents, overdoses, fight and gunshot wounds, attempted murders, and other random calamities. He is often exhausted when it's time to go home. Which, for our character Paul, is a two-bedroom apartment that he shares with his longtime girlfriend, Tiffany.

Paul grew up in an abusive household. His mother remarried when he was fairly young, and sadly, his stepfather never truly accepted him as a son. Paul's childhood was filled with constant shouting, arguing, threats to leave the family, and cruel punishments. Paul's stepfather also liked to physically hit Paul, which happened more and more until, one day, Paul finally said, "Enough!" He moved in with a kind uncle, got a job as a waiter, and saved enough money for nursing school. He swore to himself that he would never, ever allow anybody to treat him so badly ever again.

So, whenever he and Tiffany argued, it got…ugly. For example, Paul controlled their shared bank account. Since he made significantly more money than Tiffany did, he felt it was only fair to give her a weekly allowance. They often disagreed about spending, and whenever Tiffany questioned why she needed permission to buy basic life necessities (like shampoo), Paul would frown and say, "Because you are too stupid to be in control of our finances, that's why!" If Tiffany pushed the matter further, Paul would swear at her, call her awful names, and then completely go silent and refuse to talk to her for hours, or sometimes, even days!

One morning, the arguments became so heated, that Paul got drunk. He picked up his wallet and threw it at Tiffany. The leather hit her across the face, and the metal zipper cut her cheek. When she started to cry, Paul yelled at her and shook her fiercely by the shoulders, telling her to, "Be quiet, or else!" *After all, why couldn't she understand?* he thought. He was just trying to help them both! Taking care of the family finances was a man's job, and since she was too stupid to do it, the responsibility laid squarely with him. *She should be thankful,* Paul reasoned. And so it went, on and on and on.

In Love With A Monster
Life in an Abusive Relationship

Following two years of this type of quarreling, Tiffany abruptly left. She wasn't allowed to drive their car and had no money saved for a motel room, so she had a close friend come pick her up. Paul, on the other hand, was left standing at the doorway wondering, "Hey. Wait a minute. What on earth did I do wrong?" He couldn't believe it. Why did she leave?

POV: The Victim of Domestic Abuse

Tiffany loved her boyfriend Paul with all her heart. They had been high school sweethearts, dating on and off as they both pursued their chosen career paths. While Paul was successful in becoming an ER nurse, Tiffany struggled to find employment as a veterinary technician. No matter how many jobs she applied to, she could only ever secure part-time work, and so, although she didn't agree with Paul's obsession about their shared earnings, she shrugged her shoulders. When a good friend mentioned that this was a big red flag, she defended her boyfriend, figuring that it was just his odd way of showing that he cared.

But then the verbal attacks started. Paul would stomp around the apartment constantly, and he always found something to complain about that Tiffany had done wrong. Whenever she tried to explain or defend herself, Paul would scream at her. Then, the shoving happened. First, he tossed her onto the bed. A week later, into the wall. Tiffany hit her head so hard, it left a sizable bump! She really wanted to take a break, to leave for a little while...but where would she go? She was embarrassed to admit that the man she loved could act so violently, and over such small things. It was almost as if he became a totally different person when he was angry. One second, he was her loving, kind, talented boyfriend who literally saved people's lives every day! Then the next, he would get blackout drunk and transform into a monster who made her life a living Hell!

The final straw was when Paul threatened to harm their cat. Tiffany suddenly realized – she needed to get out, now! She called her best friend, packed just one bag as quickly as she could, grabbed her cat, and left. *Hopefully forever,* she thought as she slammed the door. But Tiffany knew deep down, the emotional scars wouldn't be so easy to run from...

Scenario Assessment: Types of Abuse

Phew! That was quite the story, huh? As unbelievable as it may seem, women all over the world have found themselves in similarly scary situations. After reading the tale of Paul and Tiffany, and knowing what you now know about domestic abuse, we ask: can you identify the various types of abuse taking place? Remember, abusers are experts at choosing their victims. How did Paul seek out

In Love With A Monster
Life in an Abusive Relationship

Tiffany? What power did he hold over her in their relationship? Was there empathy, mutual respect, and kindness being shown? Also, let's take a moment to recall what we have learned about the categories of abuse. Ask yourself, did you see: emotional, mental, physical, or financial abuse occurring? Hopefully, yes! All four types of abuse were present in this story. It can sometimes be hard to catch, especially when a victim is in denial about her circumstances or when the abuser is a pathological narcissist, Dr. Jekyll and Mr. Hyde type character (just like our Paul was).

However, as we said in the beginning, there may be two sides to every story. But the truth is the truth. It's not subjective. When one person uses violence, physical intimidation, threats, and mental torture to control the actions and behaviors of another human being, guess what? That's abuse.

No amount of excuses can erase this very simple fact. As this book has shown, domestic abuse is an insidious fact of life that has crept into our very homes and communities. We know it's there; many of us simply choose not to acknowledge it because admitting to the truth is much more uncomfortable than turning a blind eye and ignoring the issue. And as a result of our inaction, people die.

In Love With A Monster
Life in an Abusive Relationship

The only question left to ask is: unlike Tiffany, how many millions of women won't ever get their chance at freedom? We might never know the true number.

In Love With A Monster

Life in an Abusive Relationship

In Love With A Monster
Life in an Abusive Relationship

In Love With A Monster

Life in an Abusive Relationship

www.ingramcontent.com/pod-product-compliance
Lightning Source LLC
Chambersburg PA
CBHW030148100526
44592CB00009B/178